Student Politics in FRANCE

STUDENT MOVEMENTS—PAST AND PRESENT
GENERAL EDITOR: SEYMOUR MARTIN LIPSET

STUDENT POLITICS IN
France

A. Belden Fields

A STUDY OF
THE UNION NATIONALE
DES ETUDIANTS DE FRANCE

Basic Books, Inc., Publishers / New York / London

To Dorothy Fields, My Mother,
and to the Memory of Irving Fields, My Father,
Who Did Not Live to See This Work Completed

Preface

In 1963 and 1964, when this study was initiated, there was almost nothing on students in political science literature. It is a sign of the times that the study of students and their political attitudes and behavior is now very much in vogue.

The previous lack of attention to students in the United States is understandable, given the tone of campus life at that time. Walter Kaufman's characterization of the generation born during World War II as the "uncommitted generation" was essentially correct. "What distinguishes them," he wrote in 1960, "is that they are not committed to any cause." [1]

In a very short period this tone has undergone a radical transition. The starting point was the Berkeley Revolt of 1964.[2] Three years after the revolt led to Clark Kerr's dismissal from the presidency of the University of California, he stated: "A spectre is haunting America—the spectre of students. For the first time in the history of the United States, university students have become a source of interest for all the nation; a source of concern for much of the nation; and a source of fear for some of the nation. This is a phenomenon unique to the decades of the 1960's." [3] It is significant that these words were addressed, in March 1967, to the first international conference of scholars to deal with the subject of students and politics.

The nature of this transition in American campus life is that a significant and constantly increasing number of students are manifesting their discontent with decision-making processes or "systems," and the outputs of these systems, which regulate their lives and behavior but over which they feel they have little or no control. A sudden revaluation of patterns of authority, by any group which perceives itself as being deprived, is always felt as a threat by those who have an investment in the status quo. This occurred in the response to labor's demands for the right to organize and strike in the early part of the century, in the response to the demands of black Americans for political and social equality in the 1950's and 1960's, and in the apprehension with which student activism has been viewed since the Berkeley Revolt.

There is little doubt that so long as the United States persists in its misadventure in Vietnam the ranks of student activists will continue to swell and instances of confrontation will become progressively more serious. But even if the war were to end relatively soon, the continued toleration of racism and poverty in our society, the perpetuation of the cold war and international insecurity, and the impotence and frustration of the individual within the systems which entangle him would still continue to disturb the university communities. Thus the probabilities are very great that the phenomenon of student activism will be with us for some time to come. Furthermore, there seems to be little progress in understanding the causes and implications of that phenomenon and in thoughtfully coming to grips with them on the part of the public, elected officials, and university decision-makers. The reactions in all three sectors continue to be largely defensive and punitive. The effect of this is to provide greater disenchantment with "the system" among more people, thus further fanning the fires of confrontation. Perhaps this work, which deals with student activism in a society which has experienced it for a longer time than ours has, will contribute to a better understanding of contemporary currents in our own country. It is offered with that hope.

Our subject is French "student syndicalism" and the structure through which this concept was developed into a working doctrine, the Union Nationale des Etudiants de France (UNEF). During most of the postwar period French student syndicalism has exhibited the following characteristics: (1) a belief that the student should take an active interest both in problems of education and student life and in problems of the national and international environment; (2) a belief that a national student union should both reflect and encourage those interests; (3) strong adherence to equalitarian and libertarian values; (4) adherence to the principles of voluntary membership, active participation by the largest number of people possible, and strict control over leaders by their constituencies; (5) utilization of direct action techniques, that is, demonstrations, strikes, and rallies; and (6) a high degree of autonomy from the nonstudent political structures of the country, especially the political parties.

Chapter 1 of this study is a theoretical introduction. In it I present a typology of the kinds of student organizations in existence. The discussion is comparative, with a heavy emphasis on student organization in the areas with which I am most familiar, Europe and the United States. Second, I advance some propositions regarding the potential for the exertion of power or influence by student organizations under various conditions.

The second and third chapters are historical narrative. Chapter 2 deals briefly with student organization and activism in France up to the end of World War II. Chapter 3 is a narrative of the syndical experience from the end of World War II to the present.

The remaining chapters are descriptive and analytical in nature. Of concern will be: the factors which were conducive to student activism in postwar France; problems of formal organization, participation, and leadership; the sociology of UNEF; and UNEF, the government, and the future of student syndicalism.

The following research techniques were employed: (1) interviews with student leaders and others in French educational, political, and syndical life; (2) observation of assemblies, meetings, and demonstrations; (3) examination of the scant secondary literature; (4) collection and examination of official organizational and governmental documents and publications; (5) examination of coverage of educational affairs in the French press (especially in *Le Monde* and *France-Observateur*); (6) a questionnaire circulated to the presidents of all local chapters in the spring of 1966; and (7) my personal contact with French students as a resident of the Cité Universitaire Internationale and as a student (*auditeur libre*) at the Fondation Nationale des Sciences Politiques in Paris from September 1963 to February 1965. The questionnaire returns were poor. Of fifty distributed questionnaires, twelve were returned. On any given item no more than nine were utilizable. Almost all the data in the returns were consistent with information gained through the use of other techniques. Unless otherwise attributed, all translations from the sources which appear in the text are mine.

The field work, of course, required financing. A grant from the Council on International Relations at Yale University permitted me to do field work in France from 1963 to 1965. A subsequent trip, in June and July 1968, was made possible by grants from the Center for International Comparative Studies and the Department of Political Science at the University of Illinois, the Comparative Student Project of the Center for International Affairs at Harvard University, and the Brookings Institution. I am very grateful for this assistance.

Most sincere appreciation is extended to Professor Frederick Watkins, my adviser in the Department of Political Science at Yale University, to Professor Jean Touchard, Secretary General of the Fondation Nationale des Sciences Politiques in Paris, whose door was always open and whose kindness and wise counsel were so freely extended, and to M. Frédéric Bon of the Fondation. I am also grateful to all of those who made this study possible by graciously granting me interviews or returning questionnaires. Most of all I should like to express my gratitude and my affection to my friends and fellow students in both France and the United States; their encouragement and assistance were indispensable. Deserving of special acknowledgment are Gisèle Chemla, Laurent Chevalier, Hassane Karkar, Yvès Lépissier, Marie-Claude Perret-Gayet, Marie-Thérèse Réau, and, first and foremost, Kathryn Fields.

Urbana, Illinois   A. B. F.
March 1970

NOTES

1. Cited from Walter Kaufman, *The Faith of a Heretic,* in Howard Zinn, *SNCC: The New Abolitionists* (Boston: Beacon Press, 1964), p. 2.
2. The situation at Berkeley has been analyzed and reanalyzed. See, for example, S. M. Lipset and S. Wolin, eds., *The Berkeley Revolt* (Garden City: Anchor, 1965) and M. V. Miller and S. Gilmore, eds., *Revolution at Berkeley* (New York: Dell, 1965).
3. Clark Kerr, "From Apathy to Confrontation" (an address delivered before the Conference on Students and Politics at the University of Puerto Rico, 25 March 1967). The Conference was sponsored by the Center for International Affairs at Harvard University and by the University of Puerto Rico.

Contents

Student Politics in **FRANCE**

Chapter 1

Students as
Political Actors

It is only very recently that social scientists have become interested in student movements. Almost all of the existing literature is devoted to describing student political attitudes and trying to correlate these attitudes and behavior with sociological variables. We thus have a voluminous literature being built up by sociologists, social psychologists, and political scientists on the political socialization of students.

This literature is valuable. But it does not treat what, in the opinion of this writer, should be the central concern of political science. That central concern is political power. Too many writers simply assert in passing that students are, or have been, important in the political process, and then present the results of attitude surveys. The reader is seldom informed *how* students are influential—that is, under what conditions and through what kinds of structures students make their influence felt. This lack of attention to power and its structures is reflected in the vagueness with which the expression "student movement" is employed.

Students are, in David Truman's terminology, a categorical group.[1] A student is a person, generally between the ages of eighteen and thirty, who is enrolled in an institution of higher learning on a full-time basis. When students want to be effective—that is, exert power—they seek or form channels for articulation and action. These channels are student organizations, student interest or pressure groups; they posit certain goals which can be attained only through persuasion, threats, or coercion directed against nonstudents in policy-making positions.

A Typology of Student Organizations

Using the goals of the organization as the criterion, there are three basic types of student organizations: (1) the "student-oriented" or "corporatist" type, (2) the "environment-oriented" type, and (3) the "student and environment-oriented" type.

The Student-Oriented or Corporatist Organization

This type of organization "looks in" upon the life of the student in its academic, social, recreational, cultural and/or spiritual aspects. It is apolitical only in the sense that it does not attempt to exert influence on issues which are not directly and immediately related to these matters.

Student-oriented organizations recruit either locally (that is, at one university, campus, or *faculté*) or nationally. Examples of the former are most student government bodies at American colleges and universities. Examples of the latter are the Association of Student Governments in the United States, the National Union of Students of England, Wales, and Northern Ireland, and the Union Nationale des Etudiants de France from 1950 to 1956.

The nature of the membership can be institutional and compulsory, voluntary, or a combination. The American Association of Student Governments is an institutional association of student government leaders. If a student government decides to affiliate, a portion of each student's fees or fines goes to the organization without the student being free to opt out. Between 1950 and 1956 the Union Nationale des Etudiants de France was a voluntary, student-oriented organization. In order to join, an individual student had to request membership and purchase a membership card. The British Union represents a combination. Basically, it is an organization of participating institutions. However, if a student is enrolled in a nonparticipating institution, he may pay a fee and affiliate on an individual basis. If, however, he is a member of a participating institution, he may not opt out, and part of his fees must go toward the support of the organization.

All student-oriented groups show a high degree of independence from nonstudent hierarchies operating outside of the academic context.

The Environment-Oriented Organization

Environment-oriented organizations "look out" at the political and social environment. While they might on occasion express concern over a student-related issue, that concern is secondary.

Environment-oriented organizations can be local, national, or international. The scope of recruitment is a function of several variables: whether the organization is autonomous or affiliated with a national or international nonstudent hierarchy, the issues to which it addresses itself, the degree of centralization of the educational system, and the distance and ease of communication between institutions of higher learning.

Local environment-oriented organizations tend to be ad hoc and of short duration, arising in response to a policy over which there is severe disagreement. They also tend to arise where the educational system is decentralized and where communication between campuses is difficult. Examples are the ad hoc American student committees against the war in Vietnam.

Some national environment-oriented organizations are oriented around a single issue. An example is the Student Nonviolent Coordinating Committee in the United States, which, until its recent decision to take a position against the war in Vietnam, was concerned exclusively with the advancement of American black people. Another is the Colleges' and Universities' Campaign for Nuclear Disarmament, the student branch of the general CND in Great Britain.

Most national environment-oriented organizations, however, have more general orientations. Included among these would be student affiliates of traditional nonstudent hierarchies such as political parties and religious groups with social concerns, as well as unaffiliated ideological groups such as the left-wing Students for a Democratic Society and the right-wing Young Americans for Freedom in the United States.

In periods of international tension, associations of foreign students from the areas in crisis tend to become environment-oriented. Two of the most notable examples are the Fédération des Etudiants d'Afrique Noire en France and the Arab Students Associations in the United States.

The two major international student organizations, the International Union of Students (IUS) and the International Student Conference (ISC), are environment-oriented organizations. The IUS has served as the spokesman for the Communist Party of the Soviet Union in the international student world. The ISC was created to respond to the IUS and to compete with it for the affection of students in the newly emerging nations. The IUS is financed by communist countries and the ISC is, or was, financed covertly by the CIA. Both the IUS and the ISC, are loose associations of national student bodies. At the local and national levels, however, environment-oriented groups are voluntary associations almost without exception.

Two conflicting tendencies are apparent among an important segment of student activists in both France and the United States. The first is the desire to be effective. The second is the desire to be independent. Under conditions of political stability (that is, where the existence of the regime is not threatened by serious disagreement among nonstudent hierarchies), alienation from the system often manifests itself among students in the form of independent environment-oriented organizations. Students who join such organizations generally are serving notice to the system that they perceive it as being both morally corrupt and highly resistant to change from within the traditional structures. However, unlike the "beats" or the "hippies" who simply criticize and withdraw, they feel the need both to criticize and to make positive recommendations to society. Until very recently such organizations existed only on the right in France, the most important being the Fédération des Etudiants Nationalistes. Since 1965 such groups have been proliferating.

Students who join environment-oriented organizations affiliated with nonstudent hierarchies place a higher value upon effectiveness and advancement within the system. However, even among these the tendency to assert independence from the nonstudent hierarchies is still very strong. This often results in confrontation over moral and ideological issues. Excellent examples are the splits in 1956–1957 and in 1965 between the leaders of the Jeunesse Etudiante Chrétienne and the French Catholic hierarchy over the aims of the student group, the split from 1963 to 1965 between the leaders of the Union des Etudiants Communistes and the Central Committee of the French Communist Party over the right to disagree with the party line, and the split in 1966 and 1967 between the leaders of the College Young Democratic Club of America and the Democratic National Committee over the war in Vietnam. When serious disagreement cannot be resolved by bargaining between student and nonstudent leaders, resolution almost always takes the form of a "purge" or resignation of the student leadership.

Though the available data are statistically insignificant, I would hypothesize that the greater the degree of political instability and the newer the nation, the stronger will be the desire for effectiveness and the weaker the desire for independence. Under conditions of instability, for example in South Korea during the Rhee regime and Indonesia during the Sukarno regime, students stand a real chance of being instrumental in bringing about rapid political change if they can form alliances with or count on the support of the right nonstudent hierarchies. In both of the above countries, the support of the army was crucial. Also, in the new nations, which tend to be the least stable, the intense nationalism of students discourages political separatism. In Indonesia all the numerous environment-oriented student organizations involved in the dramatic power struggle of 1965 and 1966 were directly affiliated with nonstudent hierarchies.[2]

The Student- and Environment-Oriented Organization

This type of organization both "looks in" at the educational, social, and cultural problems of the student and "looks out" at the political and social environment. Students involved in this form of organization are interested in influencing their educational experience rather than simply imbibing it for later application as worker and citizen. But, often encouraged by society's solicitation and its benevolent image of them, these students also feel that they have something to offer the general society, not as future cadres, but presently and as students. They see themselves as the possessors of an idealism, an optimism, and a willingness to speak and to act according to true ideals. They believe their moral perspective has not been distorted by compromise with the harsh realities of adult life outside the idealistic ambiance of the university. They feel they have both a duty and a right to offer this resource to the general society.

Student- and environment-oriented organizations are almost always national. However, in countries where subnational political units of government support institutions of higher learning (for example, the United States and Canada) and/or where an important proportion of universities are private (for example, the United States and Japan), local student- and environment-oriented groups can and do arise. The students in the Free Speech Movement at Berkeley and the Waseda Movement at Waseda University, a private Japanese institution, were responding to stimuli coming from the administrations of their universities.[3] However, the issues had a political significance which transcended the immediate academic community. The same is true of the Students for Free Speech at the University of Illinois. This group was reacting to the administration's refusal to allow the DuBois Club to use university facilities and to the administration's enforcement of state legislation which places restriction on the type of speakers allowed on campus. Since the "Berkeley Revolt" there has been a noticeable increase in the militancy of some student government bodies in the United States. Several of them, including the Student Senate at the University of Illinois, have become student- and environment-oriented organizations.[4]

While national student- and environment-oriented organizations existed in totalitarian countries and in some countries in South America before World War II, there has been a remarkable postwar tendency toward the formation of such organizations, or toward the politicalization of groups previously student-oriented, in the developing areas and in western democracies. Most of the organizations referred to as "national student unions" are student- and environment-oriented organizations. The outstanding exception to this pattern in the western world is the National Union of Students of England, Wales, and Northern Ireland (NUS). In order to maintain its purity as a student-oriented organization, the NUS isolated itself from the international student world by severing its relations with the International Student Conference in 1966. However, after over two decades of almost unchallenged representation of British students, the NUS is now facing opposition from a newly created student- and environment-oriented organization, the Radical Student Alliance.[5]

Local student- and environment-oriented organizations are almost always voluntary. Indeed, the free speech movements at Berkeley and Illinois were inspired by the ideals of participatory democracy and functioned with little organizational structure. Activists would publicize open meetings in public places. The activists, who did not like to be called leaders, would attempt to get a sense of what everyone thought. Those who cared enough to come prevailed. "Members" were those who acted as such.

National student- and environment-oriented organizations can be voluntary or nonvoluntary. The Union Nationale des Etudiants de France is an example of the former. Any student in France who is not a member of the small rival union may join. National student- and environment-oriented organizations in countries which were formerly French colonies and those organizations which have anti-regimist orientations tend to be voluntary. When the organization is voluntary, membership figures provide an index to the amount of support which the organization is able to elicit; this convenience is lacking in nonvoluntary organizations.

The United States National Student Association, which has openly taken political stands since 1960, is not a voluntary organization. Its constituencies are student governments. There may or may not once have been a referendum held by the student government at a participating institution to determine whether the students then attending the institution wished to affiliate. Nevertheless, the funds a participating student government must contribute to USNSA ultimately come from the pockets of individual students. Unlike the policy of the British union, there is no provision for students at nonaffiliated institutions to join as individuals.

Varying degrees of autonomy from nonstudent hierarchies are exhibited by student- and environment-oriented organizations. National organizations' most serious problems of autonomy arise in the relationship with the government or, in the case of one-party states, with the legitimate political party. The relationships range from totally subservient organizations like the university branch of the Komsomol in the Soviet Union to openly antiregimist organizations like the Spanish Democratic University Confederation (CUDE). Many national student- and environment-oriented organizations receive financial support from their governments. This in itself, however, is not enough to indicate a low degree of independence. A low degree of independence is determined both by the degree to which an organization is dependent upon the government (or some other nonstudent hierarchy) for direct or indirect subsidization and by the extent to which the organization does the bidding of the government (or other nonstudent hierarchy) in its pronouncements and activities.

In the Soviet Union the student- and environment-oriented university section of the Komsomol is the only legitimate student organization which deals with environmental issues. Membership in the Komsomol is almost always a requirement for admission to the university.[6] The organization is tied into the political system through its subordination to the Communist Party. In the communist countries of Eastern Europe there is similarly only one legitimate student- and environment-oriented organization. However, Richard Cornell maintains that the pattern differs from the Soviet one in that only a small minority of the students actually belong to these organizations. Cornell asserts that while they do not openly oppose the party line from within and generally do not dare to form opposition groups, Eastern European students manifest their independence by resisting the pressure to join the legitimate organizations and by behaving in ways frowned upon by the Party.[7]

In Spain, on the other hand, students have dared to form a national student- and environment-oriented organization, the Spanish Democratic University Confederation (CUDE), to compete with the official Falangist student- and environment-oriented group, the Syndicate of University Students (SEU). Though the students have been beaten and placed on trial when they have tried to demonstrate, the punishment administered has been lenient (for Spain) and the organization has not been completely suppressed. One explanation which has been offered is that the students involved have come from the influential segment of Spanish society.[8] Another possibility is that the Spanish government simply does not feel secure enough to create martyrs at a time when labor unions, the lower clergy, Catalonian nationalists, and students are openly manifesting discontent with authoritarian rule. The beatings given to members of the CUDE—in the streets, on campuses, and even in churches and monasteries—have already contributed to greater militancy on the part of the other discontented elements.

From its origin in 1947 to its Congress in 1960, the United States National Student Association (USNSA) presented itself as a student-oriented organization. At the Congress of 1960, USNSA decided that it would take public stands on environmental issues. The majority of the delegates were of liberal persuasion. Conservative dissidents therefore left the association to form an Association of Student Governments. After 1960 USNSA had presented to both the American public and the external world a shining example of a "free" student union which was equalitarian and libertarian and which would not hesitate to criticize the policies of the American government where it felt that they were wrong—for example, about Vietnam.

In 1967 that image was shattered. The public, accustomed to warnings from the Director of the Federal Bureau of Investigation that the Communist Party of the United States was insidiously infiltrating American student organizations, learned that the government's own Central Intelligence Agency had covertly supplied up to 80 per cent of the yearly budget of USNSA and that some of the officers of the student organization had performed intelligence functions for the agency.[9] Despite a regular turnover of the leadership, this relationship had existed for more than fifteen years, with two or three of the top leaders of USNSA knowing about it during any given year. The continuity and secrecy of the relationship was maintained by the CIA's recruitment of former leaders of the student organization to serve as liaison agents and by threatening to prosecute under the National Security Act all student leaders who might resist and reveal the relationship.

Three factors explain how this relationship could come about in a society which considers itself to be democratic and which prizes the right of citizens to form and belong to autonomous associations. First, the early leaders of USNSA were much caught up in the ideology of the cold war and wanted to "do their part" in the world of international student politics. Their major effort went into the creation of the International Student Conference in 1950. Second, when the students approached the government for assistance in their international endeavors, the government apparently felt that giving them open assistance would arouse domestic resistance and would reduce their effectiveness in the cold war effort. What was desired were student leaders who projected an image of freedom, spontaneity, and, most blessed of all American virtues, innocence.

The last, but far from the least, important factor was the structure of USNSA. We have already indicated that it is not a voluntary organization. While it claims to act in the name of all American students, it would be surprising if one-fifth of the students in the United States even knew of USNSA's existence before its relationship with the CIA was exposed in the press.[10] Furthermore, once the national leadership is elected by a yearly congress of student government leaders and campus delegates, it is accountable to no one. When the electors return to their campuses all over the country, they, in effect, cease functioning as active members. The few national leaders and their appointed "coordinators" *are* the organization. Under these conditions, if the leadership's irreconcilable desires for effectiveness and for independence are resolved in favor of the former, the organization can easily enter a dependency relationship from which subsequent leaders will find it extremely difficult to extricate themselves.

Student Power

The expression "student power" is gaining currency in American student circles. It was inspired by the coining of the expression "black power" to signify the aspirations which the Student Nonviolent Coordinating Committee holds for another categorical, relatively powerless group in American society, the blacks. Contemporary student activists feel that they too have been deprived of influence in decision-making processes which intimately affect their lives. Now, more than ever before, they are organizing and making use of existing structures to influence these processes.

We shall here be concerned with the potential power of student organizations which are not affiliated with nonstudent hierarchies.[11] As is true for any organization composed of any category of people, the more or less immediate satisfaction of demands depends upon a multiplicity of interrelated variables. Among the most important are: the nature of the demands, the attitudes of the student body, the ability of student leadership to mobilize supporters, the attitudes of the public and other groups, and the nature of the decision-making structure.

There is no doubt that students have exercised power—that is, they have persuaded decision-makers to do what they would not have done or would have taken longer to do otherwise. In some cases they have been responsible for the removal of decision-makers who rejected their demands. But winning on a given issue is not the same as sustaining power over time. The latter requires the maintenance of an organization which is capable of regularly intervening in the policy process and winning its share of the battles. There are certain characteristics of students which render the sustained exercise of power most difficult.

First, the role of student is played only briefly in the lifespan of any given individual. The rapid rate of turnover would seem to make it difficult for a student organization to maintain itself with any degree of continuity. Indeed, there is scarcely enough time for in-group leadership training. For this reason some student organizations develop a corps of "professional" ex-student leaders. Second, students lack experience in the exercise of political skills. Engagement in a student organization generally represents their first assumption of the role of citizen. Third, students lack financial and material resources. Almost all students are financially dependent upon their parents, their university, and/or the state. Fourth, a good proportion of the student population does not possess full political rights. In most western democracies student organizations can campaign for or against candidates but do not possess a significant number of votes.[12] Fifth, students lack informal channels of access to decision-makers based upon socio-economic similarity or friendship. Sixth, students do not hold the strategic positions in society which are held by some other groups. When an army or a labor union displays its dissatisfaction with policy by withholding services, the effect upon the general society is immediate and often very grave. When students strike the impact upon society is much less immediate.

The adoption of a student and environment orientation would seem to make the leadership task even more difficult.[13] First, the adoption of general social and political positions is bound to alienate some students, potential allies, and decision-makers who might share the concerns of the organization regarding student-related issues. In no country is the student body ideologically homogeneous; to the extent that it is ideologically heterogeneous, leaders and militants must choose between broad appeal and ideological purity.

Second, questions of political ideology generally involve a greater intensity of commitment than do student-related issues. This can result in internal disagreements along narrow ideological lines which are potentially more disruptive of organizational cohesion than are disagreements over specific student-related issues. Third, the performance of the dual role means a wider dispersion of already very limited resources.

In sum, when all other variables are held constant, student organizations with a high degree of autonomy from nonstudent hierarchies would seem to be more heavily dependent upon a favorable external environment for the continuous realization of their goals than are organizations which recruit from most other social categories. Where the educational system is nationalized and/or where the organization adopts environmental goals, "favorable external environment" is likely to mean either the indulgence of political decision-makers or a high degree of political instability. The maintenance of a viable and effective student organization in the face of governmental hostility and relative political stability would appear to be a Sisyphean task.

NOTES

1. David Truman, *The Governmental Process* (New York: Alfred A. Knopf, 1951), p. 23.
2. See H. W. Bachtiar, "Indonesian Students and Politics" (paper pre-

sented at the Conference on Students and Politics, San Juan, Puerto Rico, 27–31 March 1967).

3. See Michiya Shimbori, "The Sociology of a Student Movement—A Japanese Case Study" (paper presented at the Conference on Students and Politics, San Juan, Puerto Rico, 27–31 March 1967).

4. Some of the militants in the Students for Free Speech insist that they do not care whether or not the restrictive state legislation remains on the books. Their interest is in the administration's enforcement policy. They thus attempt to keep the issue as campus-oriented as possible. This is a matter of strategy. Regardless of where the pressure is exerted, I consider the issue of free speech at a public university to have both student and environmental implications.

5. A. H. Halsey and Stephen Marks, "British Student Politics" (paper presented at the Conference on Students and Politics, San Juan, Puerto Rico, 27–31 March 1967), p. 11.

6. I should like to thank my colleague, Professor Jerry Hough, for information on the Komsomol and the universities.

7. Richard Cornell, "Students and Politics in the Communist Countries of Eastern Europe" (paper presented at the Conference on Students and Politics, San Juan, Puerto Rico, 27–31 March 1967).

8. S. M. Lipset in discussion at the Conference on Students and Politics, San Juan, Puerto Rico, 27–31 March 1967.

9. See the March 1967 issue of *Ramparts Magazine* and the Statement of the National Supervisory Board of the USNSA of 17 February 1967.

10. USNSA held its Nineteenth National Congress at the University of Illinois during the summer of 1966. Yet when this writer asked the members of his class at the University of Illinois in the fall of 1966 whether or not they knew what USNSA was, very few responded in the affirmative.

11. Student organizations which are affiliated with nonstudent hierarchies feed on the resources of the hierarchies. Much of what we shall have to say here, however, would apply to the power potential of the student affiliate vis-à-vis the nonstudent hierarchy.

12. In some American communities in which universities are located, election officials are exceedingly hesitant to register students even though they qualify. Students are often seen as an alien and potentially disruptive force in community political patterns.

13. In the language of S. E. Finer, student- and environment-oriented organizations are both "interest groups" and "promotional groups." See S. E. Finer, *Anonymous Empire* (London: Pall Mall Press, 1958).

Chapter 2

Student Organization in France before World War II

The Union Nationale des Etudiants de France (UNEF) is probably the oldest national student union in existence. The roots of the organization can be traced back to 1877, when students at the University of Nancy formed a Société des Etudiants. In the 1880's similar groups were formed in Bordeaux, Paris, and Lyon. During this decade the name Société des Etudiants gave way to the name currently in use, Association Générale des Etudiants (AGE). During the first decade of the twentieth century, AGE chapters existed at almost every French university, and a movement for the creation of a national student organization was begun. On 4 May 1907, delegates from the various AGE chapters met at Lille, and the Union Nationale des Etudiants de France was officially born.[1]

The image which the contemporary French student syndicalist holds of student culture as it existed in the late nineteenth and early twentieth centuries is most unflattering. Students of the age, including those active in the early AGE chapters, are conceived of as having been too interested in maximizing their own hedonistic delights to have been concerned with questions of polity and society. They were a small group (in 1900 France had a population somewhat in excess of 38 million and only 29,300 university students, 12,270 of whom were concentrated in Paris)[2] which, with the exception of the few scholarship students (*boursiers*) in their midst, would inherit the advantaged positions in French society. However, before these *fils à papa* accepted the responsibilities of their inheritance, they passed through a stage in which irresponsibility and amusing, "shocking" antics were acceptable to the *haute bourgeoisie*—student life.[3]

While the image of a completely apolitical student culture at the turn of the century is misleading, the historical evidence would seem to indicate that student participation in French political life was minimal during the nineteenth century. A historian who studied student involvement in the revolutions of 1848 found much material on the participation of German and Austrian students but was totally unsuccessful in finding references to French student involvement.[4] What we do find in the nineteenth century is the creation of the first "youth movements," [5] the Union Chrétienne de Jeunes Gens (about 1840) and the Association Catholique de la Jeunesse Française (about 1880).[5]

The earliest occurrences of student involvement in French political life that this writer has been able to document are related to the Dreyfus Affair. The number of students actually interested in the affair and the intensity of their commitment is obviously impossible to determine. But one need only consult the press of the epoch to confirm that the issue which brought the French professorial and literary communities into politics on a large scale also created political ferment among the student body. Much of the activity was either protesting or defending the political engagement of the professors.

For example, on 15 January 1898, after the second trial, the Latin Quarter was filled with students shouting "Down with Zola!" and "Long Live Zola!" A professor in the Faculty of Law who had taken a pro-Dreyfus position was forced to flee from his lectern when students set fire to the foot of his chair. In front of the Pantheon, which is located just across the street from the Faculty of Law, anti-Dreyfusard students danced around a fire which consumed copies of the Dreyfusard newspaper *L'Aurore*.[6]

Within the corridors of the Faculty of Letters, anti-Dreyfusard students clashed in physical combat with Dreyfusard students. Perhaps the most prominent leader of the Dreyfusard "troops" was the poet Charles Péguy, who acquired a reputation as a cane-swinging combatant.[7] If we accept Thibaudet's account of the epoch, the outnumbered Dreyfusard "troops" were mainly composed of scholarship students from the Ecole Normale Supérieure, the training ground of France's secondary and university teaching corps. The Dreyfus Affair became the symbolic issue over which the battle for the survival of the Republic was fought. An important source of recruitment for the defenders of the Republic was the academic community and the future teachers, the latter group including almost every scholarship student.[8]

The leaders of the AGE of Paris, fourteen years after its creation in 1884, entered the fray on the side of the anti-Dreyfusards. Emile Zola's "J'Accuse!" appeared in the 13 January 1898 issue of *L'Aurore*. Two days later, a reply to Zola from the governing committee of the AGE appeared in the same publication. The text reads as follows:

Monsieur,

L'Association Générale des Etudiants was deeply affected by your letter to the President of the Republic. The governing committee met immediately after its publication and decided to express to you its sad astonishment with the same frankness expressed in your appeal to the youth [of the country].

We respect every political or religious opinion and we are fervently attached to freedom of thought and expression. But we place the Army, which is the most noble expression of the homeland, and its chiefs, who are the guardians of our national honor, beyond all suspicion.

Our conscience is profoundly troubled to find such attacks delivered from the pen of a great writer who formerly, in solemn circumstances, brought us such noble and encouraging words.

Veuillez agréer, Monsieur . . .

le Comité de l'Association
Générale des Etudiants [9]

The expedition with which the meeting of the committee was called and the letter drafted and dispatched—all of this had to be done on the same day that Zola's letter appeared for the AGE's letter to have appeared on the 15th—makes it doubtful that the letter represents the first collective consideration given to political affairs by the AGE's leaders.

World War I and the economic dislocations of the interwar years were disruptive of the *belle vie* of the bourgeoisie. The universities were practically emptied during the war. In 1914 there were approximately 42,000 university students. In 1915 there were approximately 11,000.[10] After the war students from bourgeois families faced psychological, economic, and physical hardships to which they were unaccustomed. Nor were the employment prospects after graduation promising. A drastic shortage of jobs in areas related to academic disciplines, retraining of university graduates for manual labor, and a xenophobic attitude toward foreign students who came to study and, sometimes, to pursue careers in France, were unpleasant facts of French university life during the interwar period. Adding to these difficulties was the increased pressure for entrance to the university, due in large part to the institution of free secondary education in the late 1920's.[11]

Around the time of World War I, adult political organizations began to make serious appeals to the youth of the country. One source informs us that: "Only the political movements in opposition to the existing regime had important memberships; before the [Second World] War it was the Jeunesses Communistes, Socialistes, the Jeunesses Patriotiques or the young people of the Action Française."[12]

Another source minimizes the importance of the communist and socialist appeals to students before World War II:

. . . the student world was profoundly divided, especially in the political domain which interested more students than ever before. The newly created Communist Party exerted a negligible influence upon students. The Socialists, and above all the Radicals, attracted a very limited audience. The same was true of the classical Right. But two political movements were powerful: l'Action Française and le Sillon.[13] These two currents were very important. The Action Française was especially important because of the number of students that it recruited and the effectiveness of its action. It was the grand epoch, especially during the Popular Front, when Maurrasian students of the Latin Quarter dominated the faculties and the streets and administered their physical arguments. During the great confrontations between the [right-wing] leagues and the Popular Front, actual battles were fought on the Boulevard St.-Michel. Some still remember these battles between the Camelots du Roi and antifascist students and a Latin Quarter in which it was not safe to walk on certain days. The Sillon engaged in less spectacular activities which were more educational. It held meetings and demonstrations for peace and world understanding; it began the movement of youth hostels (*auberges*); it conducted welfare activities for students in difficult situations; and it conducted study and discussion sessions on the great national and international issues.[14]

From its creation in 1907, through the interwar period, UNEF devoted itself exclusively to corporate or student-related issues. Generally the approach was to study a problem, propose remedies, and seek both private and governmental action.

In response to the difficult interwar conditions and the appeals made by UNEF, an impressive set of services was provided by the state and by private donors. Perhaps most impressive was the creation of a Cité Universitaire in Paris, to provide inexpensive housing and recreational facilities for students. The French government and French and foreign private donors financed this experiment in international living.[15]

Student restaurants were established, again with both private and public funds. In 1923 the Sanatarium Saint-Hilaire-du-Trouvet was established to serve students suffering from the most widespread affliction of French students at the time, tuberculosis. Health services were also created at the Cité Universitaire in Paris and at the Universities of Nancy and Strasbourg.[16]

In 1929 the Office du Tourisme Universitaire was created to organize student voyages and to enable students to travel and vacation at lower rates. In 1933 the Bureau Universitaire de Statistiques was established to conduct research on the problem of employment for university graduates. In 1934 the Office du Sport Universitaire was created to promote physical education in France and to encourage international athletic competition. A Centre National des Oeuvres en Faveur des Etudiants was created to administer and coordinate all the programs of student assistance and services.[17] All these organizations continue to provide valuable services to the contemporary French student. As early as 1929 the value of

UNEF's initiative was accorded public recognition. The organization was declared a public service association and was awarded a state subsidy.

UNEF had a difficult time surviving World War II. Because of its association with the Third Republic, the Pétainists were dubious about the organization. At the end of 1941 a decree ordering the dissolution of UNEF was prepared. Within the threatened organization there were pressures, perhaps the strongest coming from the AGE of Montpellier, to turn UNEF into one more fascist *corporation du travail* with a national president named by the Minister of Public Instruction and local AGE secretary generals named by the recteurs of the academic districts.[18]

UNEF survived, but it was forced to bow rather low before the regime. The leadership responded to news that the dissolution decree was being considered by sending a statement to Admiral Darlan assuring him that UNEF was really an organization of the *ancien régime* but that, if the government wished to create a new student movement, the leaders of UNEF would contribute their experience to the project. At the close of UNEF's 1942 and 1943 Congresses, the organization was careful to pay its respects to Marshal Pétain. It sought to build support for itself in the regime through former members who were working in the Secrétariat Général à la Jeunesse.[19]

UNEF's fundamental occupation during the war was sending food packages and books to students in the army, in prisoner of war camps, and in German forced-labor camps. It also attempted to aid returning students in the readjustment process.[20] By a decree of 23 February 1943, all French young people became liable for forced labor in Germany. UNEF did not protest this, but contented itself with securing the most favorable conditions possible for students.[21]

From a numerical point of view the contribution of university students to the Resistance does not appear to have been very great.[22] Some students, including some UNEF leaders acting as individuals, did manifest opposition in the occupied zone. The student march on the Arc de Triomphe on 11 November 1940 was the first large-scale manifestation of resistance to the Germans in Paris. A number of the participants were killed or deported to Germany. The principal organizer of the event, a student named de Lescure, was active in UNEF. But such cases of UNEF's leaders becoming involved in resistance activity appear to have been quite exceptional.[23]

Most of the students who did participate in the Resistance did so through the channel of the Forces Unies de la Jeunesse Patriotique (FUJP), a youth alliance created in 1943 by various student and nonstudent elements interested in opposition politics. The student component of the FUJP was composed primarily of individuals affiliated with socialist, communist, progressive Christian (both Catholic and Protestant), and/or laic movements. The student division of the FUJP was concerned with basic rather than immediate problems of the student and the university. While UNEF had been interested in the provision of specific student services, the FUJP dealt with such matters as the broadening of the social base of recruitment into institutions of higher education, the right of students to "salaries," and student representation in the decision-making process within the university.[24] Their thinking paralleled the work of the resistant professors who produced the Langevin-Wallon Plan designed to render the educational system more equalitarian through structural and procedural reform at all levels.[25]

NOTES

1. Michel de la Fournière and François Borella, *Le Syndicalisme étudiant* (Paris: Editions du Seuil, 1957), p. 36.
2. *Ibid.*, p. 23.
3. See de la Fournière and Borella, *op cit.*, and Pierre Gaudez, *Les Etudiants* (Paris: Julliard, 1961).
4. Edith Altbach, "Students in the Revolutions of 1848" (paper presented at the Conference on Students and Politics, San Juan, Puerto Rico, 27–31 March 1967).
5. Conseil Français des Mouvements de Jeunesse, *Présence de la jeunesse* (Paris: Privat, 1955), p. 99.
6. *L'Aurore*, 16 January 1898, p. 2.
7. Louis Perche, *Essai sur Charles Péguy* (Paris: Pierre Seghers, 1957), pp. 30–31.
8. Albert Thibaudet, *La République des professeurs* (Paris: Grasset, 1927).
9. *L'Aurore*, 15 January 1898, p. 1.
10. De la Fournière and Borella, *op. cit.*, p. 24.
11. *Ibid.*; and Harry Van Landingham, "Special Correspondence: The

Temper of French Post-War University Life," *School and Society,* XIV, No. 353 (1 October 1921), 250–253; and "La crise et l'avenir de la jeunesse Universitaire," *Journal des Economistes* (September–October 1935), pp. 462–481.

12. Conseil Française des Mouvements de Jeunesse, *op. cit.,* p. 100.
13. The Action Française was created on 20 June 1899. Its principal doctrines were nationalism, monarchism, and anti-Semitism. The Catholic Church hierarchy was seen as an important source of support for the new political order which was advocated. The most important leaders of the movement were Charles Maurras, Leon Daudet, and Jacques Bainville. After World War I the organization was declared to be heretical by the Vatican. Although the organization was officially banned after the Liberation and some of its leaders convicted for collaboration, it continues to function in contemporary France and publishes a weekly newspaper, *Aspects de la France.* The student affiliate of the Action Française is the Etudiants de la Restauration Nationale which circulates its own newspaper, *Amitiés Françaises Universitaires* (or *A. F. Université*). The latter publication, which seems to have a very limited distribution, is extremely hostile toward UNEF.

The origin of the Sillon can be traced back to the founding of a periodical of the same name by Paul Renaudin in 1894. In 1903 one of the collaborators of Renaudin, Marc Sangnier, organized a social and political movement. The organization and the periodical were Christian humanist and democratic in orientation. Sangnier himself left the organization in 1910, after having been subjected to a papal condemnation. The Sillon no longer exists.
14. De la Fournière and Borella, *op. cit.,* p. 25.
15. Odette Pascaud, "Etudiantes de Paris," *Revue des Deux Mondes* (May–June 1935), pp. 370–375.
16. De la Fournière and Borella, *op. cit.,* p. 40.
17. *Ibid.,* pp. 40–42.
18. *Ibid.,* p. 46.
19. *Ibid.,* pp. 44–46.
20. *Ibid.,* p. 44. Also see *Un Seul Coeur* (Paris: Union Nationale des Etudiants de France, January 1944).
21. De la Fournière and Borella, *op. cit.,* 44–45.
22. No mention of student participation in the Resistance is made by the principal historian of the Resistance, Henri Michel, in his *Histoire de la Résistance en France* (Paris: Presses Universitaires de France, 1962).
23. De la Fournière and Borella, *op. cit.,* pp. 46–49.
24. *Ibid.,* p. 48.
25. *Le Plan Langevin-Wallon de réforme de l'enseignement* (Paris: Presses Universitaires de France, 1964).

Chapter 3

A History of UNEF
after World War II

From the Liberation to the Algerian War

At the Liberation, students who had participated in the FUJP formed the Union Patriotique des Organisations d'Etudiants (UPOE). This was the student affiliate of the successor of the FUJP, the Union Patriotique des Organisations de Jeunesse. UNEF was admitted to the UPOE but, because of its record during the war, enjoyed almost no influence there. According to de la Fournière and Borella, the two dominant ideological strains in the UPOE were represented by communist students and progressive Catholic students affiliated with the Jeunesse Etudiante Chrétienne.[1]

The UPOE proved disappointing to many activists in affiliated organizations. They felt its potential for action was minimal and feared it would remain a debating society. The only existing structure which looked more promising, in terms of reaching a broader segment of the student population and of potential for effective action, was UNEF. The Gaullist government had dissolved the AGE at Lyon and had confiscated its property. This provided an excellent opportunity for the ex-resistants and their allies in this capital of the Resistance to lead the way by rebuilding the AGE at the University of Lyon. True to the belief of Thibaudet, that while Paris is the literary capital of France Lyon is its political capital, the struggle to convert UNEF into a student- and environment-oriented organization was initiated in Lyon.[2]

At the first postwar Congress of UNEF, held in Dax during the Easter vacation in 1945, the Lyonnais chastised the organization for its obsequious behavior under Nazi and fascist rule. They pointed a finger of reprobation at UNEF's wartime leaders for not having taken the organization underground with other labor, teacher, and intellectual organizations. They challenged the notion that a student organization should limit its concern to the immediate problems of students qua students, as UNEF had done before the war. They urged the organization to recognize that students are citizens with social and political responsibilities to the general society, responsibilities on which UNEF had shamefully defaulted when it allowed French students to be sent to German forced-labor camps without protest or resistance and when its officers tendered their services to the fascist regime at Vichy. The only way that UNEF could restore the honor of French students and prevent a repetition of such disgraceful behavior, argued the Lyonnais, was to become attentive to its environment and active in the defense of the principles symbolized by the Resistance.

The response of the leadership was that their first responsibility had been to assure the survival of the organization and that they had been successful. This was accepted by almost all the participants except the Lyonnais. With the exception of one ex-resistant, all the members of the National Bureau (executive committee) elected by the Congress were corporatists.

The defeat of the AGE of Lyon was temporary. Its efforts were aided when, in October 1945, former combatants, prisoners of war, and deportees entered institutions of higher education. Moreover, the corporatists were embarrassed by their inability to prevail on a corporate issue—UNEF's representation on university disciplinary committees.

At the Congress of 1946 the advocates of a student and environment orientation, led by the delegates of the AGE of Lyon, Paris-Letters, and Toulouse, assumed control of the organization. This Congress, held in Grenoble, adopted for the organization a new charter, which announced that students were "young intellectual workers" with important social rights and duties.

THE CHARTER OF GRENOBLE

Adopted by the 35th Congress of UNEF *at*
Grenoble in April 1946

PREAMBLE

The representatives of the students of France, meeting in their national congress in Grenoble, April 24, 1946, conscious of the historic significance of the epoch,

In which the French Union is elaborating a new declaration of the Rights of Man and the Citizen;

In which a peaceful order among nations is being established,

In which the world of labor and youth is establishing the bases of an economic and social revolution for the benefit of mankind,

Affirm their will to participate in the unanimous effort of reconstruction,

Faithful to the traditional goals pursued by young people of the French university when they have possessed the highest degree of consciousness of their mission,

Faithful to the example of the best of them, killed in the struggle of the French for their liberty,

Noting the obsolete nature of the governing institutions,

Declare their desire to place themselves in the avant-garde of French youth as they have done so often in the course of our History, defining the bases of their work and their demands to be the following principles:

ARTICLE I. The student is a young intellectual worker.

Rights and duties of the student as a young person.

ARTICLE II. As a young person, the student has the right to special social protection in the physical, intellectual, and moral domains.

ARTICLE III. As a young person, the student has the duty to become a part of the youth of the nation and the world.

Rights and duties of the student as a worker.

ARTICLE IV. As a worker, the student has the right to work and to rest in the best conditions and in material independence, both personal and social, guaranteed by the free exercise of Syndical Rights.

ARTICLE V. As a worker, the student has the duty to acquire the best technical competence.

Rights and duties of the student as an intellectual.

ARTICLE VI. As an intellectual, the student has the right to seek the truth, and the right to freedom which is the first condition for such a search.

ARTICLE VII. As an intellectual, the student has the duty:

—to seek, propagate, and defend the Truth, which implies the duty to spread and further cultural life and to interpret the direction of the course of history.

—to defend liberty against all oppression, which is, for the intellectual, the most sacred mission.

This declaration henceforth constitutes the Charter of the Student and will serve as the preamble of the statutes of the National Union and of all the AGE's.

This text, foundation of the Student Movement, can be modified only by a process analogous to that necessary for the modification of the statutes.

The adoption of a student and environment orientation did not receive the unanimous support of the members. Opponents of the new orientation were strong enough to turn out the student- and environment-oriented National Bureau in November 1950. From November 1950 to July 1956 activists favoring a purely corporatist orientation were in the majority. During this period a two-party system developed within UNEF. Those favoring a student and environment orientation called themselves the minoritaires. In their attempt of the early 1950's to regain control of the national organization, they developed a highly structured party with an institutionalized caucus system for the formulation of policy and the making of nominations. The leaders of the caucus also exerted party discipline at congresses and assemblies and maintained a communications network between formal sessions. The majoritaires, as the corporatists were designated, did not develop the same cohesion.

During their first period of control over the organization, April 1946 to November 1950, the minoritaires* concentrated their efforts on recruiting more students into the organization and on

* While historically the term minoritaire came into use after this first period of student and environment orientation, we shall for the sake of simplicity use it to designate the leaders of that period as well as the later leaders of the same orientation. However, it will always be clear which period is under discussion.

educating the mass of students about the political and social meaning of the Charter of Grenoble. They stressed the importance of a
more equalitarian pattern of recruitment to institutions of higher
education.[3]

In the more immediate area of educational policy at the university level there were significant events. On 6–7 June 1947,
UNEF resorted to a national strike to protest government policy for
the first time in the postwar period. At issue was the budget for education, the number and size of scholarships, and the cost of rent
in the cités universitaires. On 23 September 1948, UNEF's parliamentary lobbying paid off: the legislators not only granted the students a health insurance program but also vested responsibility for
its administration in the hands of the students themselves.[4]

In the area of international student relations, the minoritaires
brought UNEF into the International Union of Students. This began
a series of battles over the international affiliations of UNEF.[5] The
headquarters of the IUS was in Prague and, in 1948 and 1949, it
consistently espoused the viewpoint of the Cominform. At the
Congress of 1949 the majoritaires were strong enough to force the
Bureau to disaffiliate UNEF from the IUS. In 1950 UNEF's Vice-
President for International Affairs attended the meeting of the IUS
as an observer. During the same summer he was one of the representatives of 22 national unions from western countries who met
in Stockholm to form a rival organization, the International Student
Conference. It is extremely doubtful that either the minoritaires or
the majoritaires suspected that the ISC was being financed by the
American Central Intelligence Agency.

The most important noncorporate issue for UNEF during this
period was colonialism. And it was the staunchly anticolonialist
stand of the IUS which attracted UNEF more than anything else.
In 1948 UNEF condemned what it called the "fratricidal war in
Vietnam." [6] The Congress of 1950 adopted a supplementary charter, the Charter of Arcachon, which called for a more responsible
policy in regard to colonial areas—including the fulfillment of
promises of emancipation made during the war. The Charter of
Grenoble was applied to students from the colonies, whose particular mission was defined as participation "in the efforts of their
countries to achieve emancipation within the framework of the
French Union!" [7]

The majoritaires assumed power in November 1950. Relations with the ius were totally severed. The majoritaires did not initiate any radically new policies, even in the corporate realm. Indeed, in at least one instance, they resolutely defended what had been gained. When the appropriations of the student insurance fund were in danger of being reduced as an economy measure, the majoritaire Bureau called the second postwar national strike on 15 March 1951. The majoritaires, however, were usually more inclined to compromise with the government than to oppose it with direct action techniques. Attacking the majoritaires for lack of initiative and timidity when dealing with the government, the minoritaires succeeded in gaining access to the National Bureau in July 1953 as the minority partner in a coalition.

During the coalition period, from July 1953 to July 1956, the more aggressive minoritaires made their presence felt. Four different national strikes and/or demonstrations were held to protest the insufficiency of the government's expenditures in the field of education. Again UNEF was to win a major parliamentary victory when a law of 17 April 1955 gave statutory recognition and endowment to the Centre National des Oeuvres en Faveur de la Jeunesse Scolaire et Universitaire (CNO). The law provided that the "most representative student associations" were to share the responsibility for decision-making and administration in the area of student services with representatives of the Ministry of Education. The Administrative Council of the CNO was to be composed of six representatives appointed by student associations, five representatives selected by the Minister from a list of fifteen nominees submitted by student associations, and twelve representatives from the Ministry of Education or selected by the Minister.[8]

The satisfaction of UNEF's corporate demands was largely the result of the good relations UNEF had established with the Education Committee of the Chamber of Deputies. While close relations with the Ministry of Education were valued and maintained during the ministries of Depreux (1948), Marie (1952), and Billières (1957–1958),[9] the securing of demands which involved increased public expenditures required legislative lobbying during the Fourth Republic.

Not all of UNEF's corporate demands were granted, however. Aside from its unchanging belief that the education budget was too low, the major defeat suffered by UNEF was its inability to induce the legislature to establish a scholarship program which would render all students financially independent (the présalaire, subsequently referred to as the allocation d'études). In 1950 the Education Committee of the Chamber of Deputies unanimously approved the proposal. When the bill came to the floor in 1951, it was opposed by the Ministry of Finance and went down to defeat.[10] Chiffre, without mentioning specifics, maintains that UNEF played an especially active role in the legislative elections of 1955 and 1956. Nevertheless, the newly elected legislature rejected the proposal in 1956 and 1957.[11]

UNEF and the Algerian War

The postwar issue which was to have the most important impact upon UNEF was the Algerian War.[12] It was first debated at the opening of the academic year 1955–1956. At an intense session of the General Assembly in October, the majoritaire Bureau was voted out of office on the issue. A minoritaire president, François Borella, was elected, but the situation was so unstable that his Bureau fell a few hours after it had been elected. For fifteen days UNEF was forced to exist without a national president. After the cooling-off period, a majoritaire president was invested.

At the Congress held in April 1956, the minoritaires were strong enough to secure the right officially to observe the meetings of the International Union of Students, recognition of the student unions of Tunisia and Morocco, and the maintenance of relations with the uncompromisingly nationalistic Union Générale des Etudiants Musulmans Algériens (UGEMA). However, their candidate for the presidency, Michel de la Fournière of Paris-Letters, narrowly missed being elected. Nevertheless, support of the majoritaire Bureau which was elected by the Congress was so tenuous that the Bureau fell at the next general assembly in July. In July 1956 the investiture of a Bureau presided over by de la Fournière initiated a period of minoritaire control which has lasted up to the present writing. Although there were threats of secession from the ranks by the majoritaires, the only AGE not to recognize the new Bureau when the school year began was that of Algiers. Dominated by non-Arabs favoring an *Algérie française*, it disaffiliated from UNEF.[13]

On 4 November 1956, approximately four months after it had taken control, the minoritaire Bureau received from the Hungarian Youth Union an appeal for support in its struggle against the Soviet Army. The Bureau responded with three measures. It issued a "salute to the students killed in the struggle for freedom." [14] It addressed a message to the International Union of Students expressing astonishment at the silence of that organization. And it asked Soviet students to postpone a long planned France-Soviet Week. These actions were ratified almost unanimously by UNEF's Conseil d'Administration.[15]

On December 10 the UGEMA asked UNEF to be as unequivocal about its support for "the aspirations of the Algerian people" as it had been about its support of the Hungarians. De la Fournière, in a frank letter of December 26, explained that while a vast majority of French students were in agreement on the Hungarian question, there was deep division on the question of Algeria and thus a declaration of firm support was simply impossible at the time.[16] As a result the Algerian union broke all ties with UNEF on 2 January 1957. All nonmetropolitan and non-French AGE's in the French Community joined the UGEMA in its action. Relations with the UGEMA were to remain severed until 1960.

From 1957 to 1960 the Algerian War was discussed at every UNEF Congress, but the minoritaire leadership did not possess the strength to commit the organization to a position. When, at the Congress of 1957, the minoritaires proposed sending a letter to the president of the Republic calling for negotiations, delegations from seventeen AGE chapters walked out. This was despite the minoritaire leadership's offer to concede on the question. Eight of the most adamant AGES formed a rival union, the Mouvement des Etudiants de France et de l'Union Française pour la Réunification de l'UNEF (MEF). The government encouraged the dissidents to re-enter UNEF in January 1958, which they finally did in November.[17]

Chiffre maintains that some pressure had developed in the government for the recognition of the MEF, but that it was resisted by the Minister of Education, René Billières, who sent a representative to the Marseilles Congress.[18] While such pressures may have existed, the most serious confrontations between UNEF and the government were to occur under the Gaullist regime which came into being approximately two weeks after the Congress met.

From the very beginning of the Gaullist regime, UNEF and the government came into conflict. Without taking a position on the substantive problem of the war, UNEF began to demonstrate for the preservation of civil liberties. It opposed the government's plan to create a separate Ministry or Commissariat of Youth, although a solution acceptable to UNEF was worked out when the government agreed to attach the Commissariat of Youth to the Ministry of Education. They also came into conflict with the government by supporting reform proposals advocated by Minister of Education Billières. De Gaulle rejected the proposals and Billières subsequently resigned. Chiffre maintains that de Gaulle deliberately chose 10 December 1958, a day on which UNEF had been holding demonstrations, to respond to the National Bureau support of Billières' proposals. He quotes the following passage from de Gaulle's letter: "I cannot accept the proposition that the President of UNEF is in any position to speak to me of shortcomings." [19]

Despite this initial hostility, UNEF did not take an antagonistic position during the constitutional referendum of September. Some of the teachers' syndicates affiliated with the Fédération de l'Education Nationale had advocated rejection of the constitution and the Gaullists. Similarly, the government apparently did not attempt to play upon UNEF's difficulties with its dissident majoritaires. On the contrary, M. Herzog, the Gaullist High Commissioner for Youth and Sports, is credited with encouraging the dissidents to return to the ranks; the minoritaires had conceded them nothing. The terms of the "agreement" (15 November 1958) by which the dissidents returned were as follows:

> . . . student syndicalism recognizes as its end and as its limit the study and the solution of problems directly concerning the student as he is defined by the fundamental Charter of the Movement.[20]

While taking no overall position on the war itself, UNEF did protest specific policies directly connected with the war. In 1958 UNEF opposed the government's banning of the Algerian Arab students' union. At the Congress of 1959 the organization protested what it considered to be illegal treatment of Arab students; [21] the motion of protest was proposed by majoritaires who warned against exploiting such protest for "political" ends. Their motion was accepted by the Congress, but the minoritaires presented a second motion hinting at negotiations between the French and the FLN. The majoritaires left the hall and the second motion was also adopted. This time, however, there was no question of a new secession. [22]

The most crucial affair of 1959 came about several months after the Congress had adjourned. On 11 August 1959, the Minister of the Army issued a decree drastically limiting the granting and renewal of draft deferments. Now for the first time the war threatened to intrude upon the lives of a substantial number of students in immediate and corporate terms. Thus the corporatist AGE of Paris-Science was in the vanguard of those urging that UNEF take action against the ministerial order.

UNEF contested the decree before the Conseil d'Etat and defended students affected by it before the Conseils de Révision, roughly the French equivalents of American selective service review boards. It won most of the cases. UNEF combined its appeals to adjudication with pressure tactics. It contacted the offices of the premier and parliamentary deputies; it threatened to withdraw from the Commission Armée-Jeunesse (an advisory committee designed to foster good will between the armed forces and the country's youth); and, after the government banned a meeting to be held on 8 March 1960, it struck on the 15th and the 16th. The pressure tactics were successful, and a deferment policy acceptable to UNEF was announced on March 17. [23]

The minoritaires were becoming increasingly impatient to take a forthright position on the war itself. A major aim of the leaders was to develop a united syndical front of workers, teachers, and students (*intersyndicalisme*) to oppose the war.

UNEF had been developing closer relations with the corporate- and environment-oriented teachers' unions since 1958. Beginning in August of that year they had participated together in the Groupement d'Etudes et de Rencontre des Organisations de Jeunesse et d'Education Populaire (GEROJEP), a group of fifty-three organizations which had joined together to oppose the creation of an autonomous Ministry of Youth.[24] They had since met regarding various educational problems. UNEF's 1959 adoption of a position favoring *laïcité* (separation of church and schools), a subject which was not of very keen interest to the minoritaires, was clearly intended to facilitate closer relations between UNEF and the large, aggressive teachers' union, the Fédération de l'Education Nationale (FEN). Early in April 1960 the secondary and technical teachers' affiliates of the FEN called for establishment of a permanent committee to work for an Algerian peace. The Syndicat Général de l'Education Nationale (the SGEN, an affiliate of the CFTC) called for a strong syndical front with liaison committees at the regional level.

The minoritaire leaders had also begun to renew contact with the leaders of the Algerian Arab student union which had reconstituted itself in Tunis. Informal negotiations were undertaken in November 1959, and further negotiations occurred at the meeting of the Executive Council of the International Union of Students held in Tunis in February 1960.[25] As they had before the break in relations in 1957, the Algerian students pressed for a clear statement of support for the aspirations of Algerian nationalists.

At their own Congress of 1960 the minoritaires decided to force the issue. A motion calling for a cease-fire and for negotiations with the FLN, based upon French recognition of the right of self-determination, was passed by a large majority. In May and June, Dominique Wallon, the newly elected Vice-President for International Affairs, met with leaders of the Algerian union in Lausanne, Switzerland. Relations between the two student organizations were reestablished and, on June 6, a joint communiqué was issued which echoed the call of the April Congress for negotiations with the FLN and self-determination for Algeria.[26]

UNEF's engagement was gradual and recognized definite limits. Therefore, the relatively moderate leadership was challenged by activists who felt UNEF did not go far enough and by the government and majoritaires who felt UNEF went too far.

A series of underground networks was formed to aid the FLN in metropolitan France. Perhaps the best known of these was led by Francis Jeanson, a collaborator of Jean-Paul Sartre on *Les Temps Modernes*.[27] Some students were attracted to these support networks. In June 1960 six students were arrested and charged with complicity. Of these six, four were UNEF activists at the local level: a president and a former president of the AGE of Scientific Preparation, and the president and treasurer designates of the minoritaire opposition at the Institute of Oriental Languages. The majoritaire president of the AGE at the Institute attacked UNEF's national leadership, asserting that this sort of behavior was the logical consequence of their policies and that they were as guilty as those arrested.[28]

The leadership was extremely fearful that the entire student movement might be compromised. On June 14 the National Bureau issued a communiqué disavowing "desperate violence." On the 16th a special General Assembly was convened at which it was declared that the reestablishment of relations with the Algerian student union was an attempt to encourage the substitution of dialogue for war and that it did not imply that UNEF accepted all of the positions of the UGEMA. UNEF members were asked not to extend active assistance to the FLN.

In June the Minister of Education, Louis Joxe, sent a letter to the National Bureau, informing it that UNEF's subsidy was therewith suspended. Four months later, at the beginning of the 1960–1961 school year, the government sought personal retribution against Dominique Wallon, Vice-President for International Affairs. On October 18 he was informed that his draft deferment had been revoked. This measure, however, was successfully challenged through adjudicative procedures.

Also in June the majoritaires consolidated their forces. On June 6 the more alienated majoritaire AGE leaders created the Comité de Liaison et d'Information des Etudiants de France (CLIEF). It condemned the Algerian policy of the minoritaires and urged the government to initiate a subsidy directly to the local AGE chapters, to prevent the National Bureau from doing "further harm to France." [29] At the same time the leaders of the CLIEF made it plain that theirs was not a secessionist movement. Indeed, not every majoritaire AGE took part in the CLIEF. At the General Assembly in July, the majoritaire AGE of Paris-Pharmacy presented a motion simply protesting the government's termination of the subsidy.

The termination of the subsidy did not bring the operations of the national organization to an immediate halt, because the subsidy accounted for only about 25 per cent of its revenue. The rest was extracted from local membership dues. But operations were rendered more difficult. In an attempt to minimize the impact of the loss, the National Bureau borrowed money from cooperative local chapters and from such external organizations as the Confédération Générale du Travail (CGT), the Ligue Française de l'Enseignement, the Fédération de l'Education Nationale (FEN), and the FEN's largest affiliate, the Syndicat National des Instituteurs. Some gifts were also forthcoming from anonymous sources.[30]

Although some more moderate majoritaire AGE's were sympathetic with the National Bureau, others (for example, Montpellier) attempted to further undercut the financial status of the national by buying few membership cards. The AGE's of Nice and Paris-Law ceased selling national membership cards entirely, broke all relations with the National Bureau, and were expelled from UNEF.[31]

The financial assistance which came from other syndical organizations was the result of joint political action. Between 28 May 1958 and 12 March 1962, UNEF engaged in eleven national strikes and/or demonstrations in defense of republican institutions and individual liberties and/or against the war. In seven of these instances UNEF was acting in coordinated efforts with workers' and/or teachers' syndicates. While UNEF, in line with its policy of intersyndicalism, was greatly interested in developing working relationships with the teachers' FEN and the workers' CGT, the two most powerful syndicates in their own spheres of activity, the traditional animosity and lack of trust between the two made joint positions and unified action extremely difficult. Moreover, the Confédération Générale du Travail-Force Ouvrière (CGT-FO) generally wanted no part in any action in which the Confédération Générale du Travail (CGT) was involved. The Confédération Française des Travailleurs Chrétiens (CFTC) would not engage in joint action with the CGT unless the CGT-FO or the Fédération de l'Education Nationale (FEN) was also involved. In the fall of 1960 UNEF found itself in a circle of traditional intersyndical hostility.

UNEF also made contact with the Algerian labor movement through the Algerian student union. A joint statement was issued by UNEF, the UGEMA, and the Algerian Workers' Union, calling for a cease-fire, negotiations, self-determination without partition, and guarantees of individual liberties. The statement was ratified by the CGT and the Syndicat Général de l'Education Nationale of the CFTC. The essentials were incorporated into the positions of the CFTC and the CGT-FO. The FEN called for the "reasoned adherence of all interested parties." [32]

The Congress of 1961 was held during the last week of April, a period of extreme political tension. France was bracing itself against the prospect of the military coup in Algeria extending itself to the mainland. The minoritaires retained their control and Dominique Wallon was elected president of UNEF. In response some majoritaire AGE's called for a modification of UNEF's organization which would give greater power to the *offices*, the structures of UNEF which group students according to general areas of study. Their sole function is to advise the organization on problems related to their areas of academic study. Since the most determined opposition to the policy of the minoritaires lay in the six professional and commercial schools, which outnumber the three *offices* of letters, science, and pre-university preparation, strengthening the power of the *offices* would have amounted to strengthening the power of the majoritaires.

In fact, a second schism had already begun in UNEF. In March the *office* of students in medicine, except for six medical schools of minoritaire orientation (Paris, Caen, Amiens, Nancy, Strasbourg, and Grenoble), created the Union Nationale des Etudiants en Médecine which was totally independent of UNEF. The medical organization declared itself "apolitical" and elected Jean-Marie Llapasset of Montpellier as its president. After the Congress refused to grant the demanded increase in power to the *offices*, students in commerce, dentistry, and law followed the example of the medical students. [33]

The schism resulted in the creation of a rival organization which had the blessings and the assistance of the government. On May 27 the Minister of Education, Lucien Paye, delivered an ultimatum to UNEF's Bureau. If within ten days the members of the Bureau did not sign a pledge stating that they would not take political positions, the Ministry would "find others with whom to deal." [34]

The Bureau refused. In June students in the professional *offices* who had broken away from UNEF in the spring met at Montpellier to form a rival student organization, the Fédération Nationale des Etudiants de France (FNEF). Llapasset, the president of the Union Nationale des Etudiants en Médecine, was elected to the presidency of the FNEF. Also in June, students in commercial and technical schools formed an organization to rival the UNEF-affiliated Union des Grandes Ecoles.[35] This new organization, the Fédération Nationale des Associations d'Eleves en Grandes Ecoles, did not officially affiliate itself with the FNEF.

Even before the FNEF was officially organized, the government awarded it a state subsidy while continuing to withhold UNEF's. The government also awarded to the FNEF two of UNEF's appointed seats on and one nomination to the Administrative Council of the CNO. It continued its personal vendetta against Wallon by attempting to prevent him from sitting on the Council and by refusing to allow him to sit for the entrance examination of the Ecole Nationale d'Administration.[36] Wallon gained personal relief through adjudication and, in November 1963, the Tribunal Administratif of Paris ruled that the award to the FNEF of a portion of UNEF's representation on the CNO was illegal, because the FNEF was not "representative at the time." [37] This decision, though a moral victory for UNEF, was of little practical value, because a ministerial decree had modified the representational scheme of the CNO one month before the decision was rendered.[38]

During the fall and winter of the academic year 1961–1962, UNEF was busily engaged in an attempt to bring the labor and teachers' unions together in a common demonstration of opposition to the war and to the terroristic acts of the colonialist Organisation de l'Armée Secrète (OAS). During the winter these acts had become alarmingly frequent in Paris. One reaction to OAS activity in metropolitan France had been the formation of "antifascist" committees. Within the university community the Front Universitaire Antifasciste had been created.

The national leaders of UNEF feared the powers of attraction of this virulent antifascist movement, especially in certain Parisian AGES: Literary and Scientific Preparation, Medicine, Letters, and the Ecole Normale Supérieure. The national organization remained aloof from the Front. It continued to play a more temperate role, trying to unify syndical demonstrations in favor of termination of the war and of resistance to all attempts by the OAS or the Army to seize power or to employ violence in metropolitan France. The reason for this aloofness was that the national leaders were wary of the heavy participation of the Communist Party and of individuals inclined toward violence in the "antifascist" movement. In January some Parisian activists in UNEF, who were also associated with the antifascist movement, took part in a raid on the FNEF's office at the School of Law. At the General Assembly of February, UNEF's leaders warned the membership against compromising the "freedom of judgment and decision of the movement. . . ." [39]

Ironically, the syndicates were able to come together for common action only one month before the war was actually terminated. On February 8 a series of bombings was perpetrated in Paris, presumably by the OAS. All major syndical organizations except the CGT-FO, plus the Communist Party and the Parti Socialiste Unifié, participated in a demonstration against the activities of the OAS. The consequences of this demonstration and of the attempt by the government to squelch it were particularly tragic. The police, or paramilitary Compagnies Républicaines de Sécurité (C.R.S.), chased some of the demonstrators to the Métro Charonne. As the pursued attempted to descend the stairs of the station, the police charged forward. Some maintain that they actually pressed the mass of humanity with iron grilling.[40] Nine people were crushed or suffocated to death.

The reaction on the left was shock and anger. On February 13, the day of the burial of the victims of Charonne, the Parisian section of the CGT-FO joined representatives of the other syndicates to which UNEF had been appealing in a memorial service followed by a general work stoppage.[41] On March 12 another work stoppage was held to protest further OAS attacks.

During the period of the Algerian War UNEF did not completely ignore educational problems; it was especially vocal about budgetary appropriations. However, between the advent of the Fifth Republic and the end of the Algerian War in April 1962, the life of the organization virtually revolved around the conflict and the related problems of threats by the military, OAS terrorism, and protecting

the rights of opponents to the war. Upon the granting of independence to the Algerians, these issues became history.

UNEF after the Algerian War

At the Congress of April 1962 the minoritaires, who emerged
from the Algerian War in complete control of the national organization and of nearly every AGE, focused their attention almost exclusively upon problems of education and student welfare. Three
months later, at the General Assembly of July, their newly elected
president was turned out of office and replaced by their vice-
president for university affairs. No environmental issues were involved in the dispute, which centered on the problem of what
position to take on the question of student housing. The new
president, Jean-Claude Roure, devoted most of his energies to an
attempt to reestablish relations with the Ministry of Education.[42]

The Ministry itself was undergoing a change in personnel. Lucien
Paye, who had been involved in the imposition of sanctions against
UNEF during the war, was replaced as Minister of Education in
April 1962 by Pierre Sudreau. In December M. Sudreau was himself replaced by Christian Fouchet. In February 1963 M. Fouchet
refused to receive a delegation from the National Bureau. UNEF
demonstrated in protest, and the delegation was received approximately three weeks before the Congress of 1963. The Minister
refused to make any concessions on the reestablishment of relations or the resumption of the subsidy.

The National Bureau also entered into an agreement with representatives of the teachers' unions to hold a twenty-four-hour strike
on April 25 to protest what they considered to be insufficient
budgetary allocations to education. That dissatisfaction over the
allocations was widespread is indicated by the fact that even the
FNEF supported the strike.

The Congress of 1963 was attended by representatives of the
Ministries of the Army and Foreign Affairs and by the Director
of the Centre National des Oeuvres, but not by representatives of
the Ministry of Education. M. Roure admitted that his Bureau had
been unsuccessful in opening channels of access to the Ministry or
in gaining any concessions. However, he urged the delegates to

remain temperate and to resist the appeals and temptations to an antiregimist political campaign. Although the moderate Roure had been elected by a very large majority in 1962, his report to the 1963 Congress was accepted by a narrow margin. And the Vice-President for University Affairs in the previous Bureau, Michel Mousel, encountered a very serious challenge from an "anti-Gaullist" candidate in his bid for the presidency.

Mousel ran on a platform entitled "La Voie Universitaire" ("The University Path"). His Bureau was committed to devoting its attention to the reestablishment of relations with the Ministry and to the improvement of the living and working conditions of the students. The three major areas of concern were scholarships, student housing, and structural and pedagogical reform. Approximately two weeks after Mousel's election, M. Fouchet restored UNEF's subsidy.

If the Minister rewarded UNEF with a carrot at the end of the academic year 1962–1963, he greeted the students with a stick at the beginning of the next academic year. In October 1963 M. Fouchet issued a ministerial decree designed to insure his firm control over the Centre National des Oeuvres. The ratio of government to student representatives on the Administrative Council of the CNO was changed from 12:11 to 15:7. Student associations were given the right to name seven representatives, one more than under the provisions of the 1955 law, but their right to nominate additional representatives was revoked. Of the seven student seats, four went to UNEF and the remaining three were awarded to the FNEF, the UGE, and the FNAGE. Furthermore, while the director of the CNO had previously been named by the Minister from a list of three to six names presented to him by the Administrative Council, the decree stipulated that the Minister would henceforth assume a completely free hand in the selection of the director.[43]

The ceremony celebrating the reopening of the Sorbonne for the academic year was set for November 7. M. Fouchet was to present honorary degrees to a group of eminent international scholars. But the AGE of Paris-Letters (the Sorbonne) called upon students to express their grievances in a mass demonstration. As precautionary measures the government stationed a large police force around the Sorbonne, and erected barricades one block from the entrances which only those with invitations for the ceremony were permitted to pass. Students milled about outside the perimeter waiting for Fouchet's car.

The Minister did not appear. Without notice to the participants in the ceremony, he had sent the Secretary of State for Sports and Youth, M. Herzog, in his place. This provoked the Rector to make several biting remarks during the ceremony about the government's lack of concern for education. This spectacle was viewed by all the honored scholars, university administrators and faculty members, members of the diplomatic corps, and some foreign students.

It was only when the ceremonies ended at noon that the students outside the Sorbonne learned of Fouchet's absence. They began to shout: "Fou-chet Dé-mis-sion!" ("Resign Fouchet!") and "Des Am-phis! Pas de Can-nons!" ("Classrooms! Not Guns!"). There was some jostling between the police and students. A student was reported to have knocked the cap off the head of an officer, and some students were reported to have thrown mud and rocks at the police. The police charged with clubs and leaded capes, barricades were thrown back and forth, and several students were hurt, apparently none very seriously.[44]

The students marched three blocks up Boulevard St.-Michel to UNEF's offices on rue Soufflot. There Michel Mousel, the president of UNEF, addressed the students: "This demonstration is only a warning of much larger ones to come. We shall return ten times more numerous." [45] The president of the AGE at the Faculty of Letters said: "We have not seen so many people since the demonstrations over Algeria. If we are 4,000 or 5,000 at the beginning of the year, we shall soon be 10,000. All of you come back in ten days with one or more friends." [46] The entire demonstration lasted for perhaps forty-five minutes.

The invitation to return in ten days was in reference to a "Week of Action" which was being planned by UNEF and the university teachers' union affiliated with the FEN, the Syndicat National de l'Enseignement Supérieur. Also associated with the enterprise were four other unions attached to the FEN and the Syndicate Général de l'Education Nationale (SGEN), an affiliate of the CFTC. The FNEF supported the action but remained isolated from the other groups.

The "Week of Action" extended from the 21st through the 30th of November. On the 21st UNEF and the Syndicat National de l'Enseignement Supérieur held a press conference to explain what was being demanded. In their presentation the leaders of the Syndicate demanded: an increase in the education budget for the construction of more facilities, for the creation of a "sufficient" number of faculty positions, and for enlargement of the subvention funds given to French academics for research to 30 per cent of the base salary; cancellation of the projected plan to administer parallel examinations for the degrees of *agrégation* and CAPES for teachers in private schools; [47] and the cancellation of a ministerial decree giving increased powers to *préfets coordonateurs* (representatives of the national government operating in the local districts), especially the power to nominate rectors of universities.[48]

The president of UNEF supported the demands of the Syndicat National de l'Enseignement Supérieur and articulated a separate list of demands for UNEF. He called for an additional 500 million franc investment (approximately 100 million dollars) in education within a two-year period. The money was to be spent to hire more faculty members, to construct more facilities, to stimulate research, to increase scholarship stipends by 10 per cent, to create 12,500 new scholarships (rather than the 6,500 proposed in the budget), and to enlarge the funds already appropriated for ongoing expansion programs (*crédits de paiements*) from 796 million francs to 950 million francs.[49]

M. Mousel made three further demands. First, he called upon the government to open negotiations with UNEF over the problem of the reform of higher education. Second, he called upon the government to grant all students sustaining scholarships (the allocation d'études), beginning with students already possessing the first degree (*licence*) and students in the grandes écoles. Third, he called for the general institution of small work groups or class sections, which would permit greater individual attention.[50] It was also made clear that the "Week of Action" was a protest against the ministerial decree reducing student participation on the Administrative Council of the CNO.

The "Week of Action" involved six days of strikes by students and faculty members amid a massive publicity campaign. The actual number of days that students and faculty members in any given institution struck varied. All UNEF chapters and sections in letters and science struck for the full six days. In Paris the AGE's of medicine and the Ecole Normale Supérieure struck for the full six days, the chapters at the Institut d'Etudes Politiques and the Ecoles des Hautes Etudes Commerciales for three days, and those at other grandes écoles for two days.[51] Medical, law, and technical or engineering students in at least fourteen provincial universities struck for varying durations.[52]

Newspaper reports on the first day of the strike indicated that the call to strike was effective. Almost 100 per cent of the students in letters and science and 100 per cent of the members of the Syndicat National de l'Enseignement Supérieur respected the strike. According to these reports all of the *assistants* and *maîtres assistants* (junior faculty members) struck at Strasbourg, Grenoble, and Toulouse. All of the law students at Grenoble, Dijon, and Toulouse were reported to be on strike, as were about 75 per cent at Nancy. On the other hand the response was poor among the students at the Faculty of Law in Paris.[53] At the schools of medicine the strike call was reported to be 100 per cent successful among students in Paris, Grenoble, and Lyon, 100 per cent successful among the faculty members in Grenoble and 80 per cent effective among the professors in Strasbourg. In the grandes écoles 100 per cent compliance was reported at the Ecoles Normale Supérieure in Paris and in the grandes écoles of Besançon, Grenoble, Nancy, Nantes, Poitiers, Strasbourg, and Toulouse.[54]

On the third day of the strike UNEF and the Syndicat National de l'Enseignement Supérieur announced at a news conference that, despite the abstention of the nonactivist Fédération des Syndicats Autonomes de l'Enseignement Supérieur (with approximately 7,000 members, the largest teachers' union at the university level), 65 per cent of the teaching staff in faculties of letters and science was respecting the strike. They claimed that only 10 per cent of the classes and work sessions in these faculties were being held.[55]

Undoubtedly, part of the success of the strike was due to the use of pickets. UNEF had announced that it would station pickets at the entrances of academic buildings. The pickets were to explain the reasons for the strike and to attempt to convince students to respect it. At the Sorbonne, however, the pickets physically barred access to the building. This was confirmed both by Bertrand Girod de l'Ain, education editor of *Le Monde,* and by this writer. When Girod de l'Ain questioned the pickets at the Sorbonne, he was told: "We are explaining that entrance is forbidden." [56]

From the second day of the strike there were instances of police interference with the activities of the militants. A vice-president of the AGE at Paris-Letters and another activist were arrested for posting stickers publicizing the strike and demonstration. Two law students were arrested for distributing tracts to students entering the Lycée Montaigne for night work sessions. On the 28th the president and several members of the AGE at Paris-Letters were arrested for forbidding access to students enrolled in night courses there. They were released when approximately 100 students and several professors protested the arrest at the commissariat.[57]

Included in the plans for the "Week of Action" was a demonstration to be held on the last day. On Friday, November 29, students and teachers were to assemble for a meeting outside UNEF's offices on rue Soufflot and then to march to the Faculty of Science. In conformity with the law, UNEF and the Syndicat National de l'Enseignement Supérieur sent a letter to the Préfet of Paris informing him of their plans. The Préfet responded that

> . . . because of the constantly increasing problem of traffic, parades on the public roads and meetings of persons and demonstrations in the public ways can no longer be authorized when they are of such a nature as to disturb the public tranquility and to be a nuisance to the life of the people of Paris. You will note that the demonstration which you propose to organize fits this description.
>
> Consequently, I can extend permission neither for a meeting in front of the headquarters of the Union Nationale des Etudiants de France . . . nor for a march to the Faculty of Science.
>
> The interested organizations will be held responsible if they violate this decision.
>
> However, I should have no objection to a meeting in a hall of your choice, in an enclosed area, out of the public way.[58]

The Syndicat National de l'Enseignement Supérieur protested the decision of the Préfet but did hold its demonstration in the courtyard of the Institut Poincaré. Under a banner reading "Five

Years of Promises," representatives of local unions affiliated with the three major labor confederations expressed the solidarity of the workers with the academics. The President of UNEF also addressed the assembly.[59]

UNEF, however, decided to defy the ban and to hold the demonstration and march as planned. The police placed several thousand men in the fifth and sixth *arrondissements*. A cordon was thrown up to keep students out of the areas bounded on the east by rue St.-Jacques, on the west by Boulevard St.-Michel, on the south by rue Auguste-Comte, and on the north by the Quai. Standing by to support the police were members of the paramilitary Compagnies Républicaines de Sécurité, motorcycle men from the gendarmerie, and a tank designed to shoot water at high pressure.

Scattered clashes occurred outside the cordon. At approximately 4 P.M. a group of about 2,000 students broke the cordon at rue Auguste-Comte. Once the cordon was broken students gained access at other points. The students chanted for Fouchet's resignation and for classrooms rather than guns. Police officers, attacking in groups, attempted to isolate students and then beat them with leaded capes. Although one police officer was hospitalized, this observer noted no instance of students attacking a police officer. Once the police lines were broken the students were willing to content themselves with chanting and attempting to outrun the pursuing police.

Several students were injured and approximately 150 were arrested. On December 2 a hearing was held before a police magistrate, to determine whether legal action should be instituted for violation of the prefectoral ban on the demonstrations. The president of UNEF disclaimed his organization's responsibility by maintaining that, after the ban, UNEF took no action to provoke meetings anywhere in the Latin Quarter.[60] Five days after the hearing the president issued a press release in which he asserted that, since the National Bureau had not called off the demonstration, it was assuming full "moral" responsibility. Girod de l'Ain, one of UNEF's staunchest supporters, administered paternal chastisement in the pages of *Le Monde* because UNEF did not assume responsibility.[61] No legal action was taken against UNEF.

The "Week of Action" was given much publicity in the written media. Newspapers and magazines were filled with articles on students and on the problems of higher education, despite the death of President Kennedy that very week. The press—both Communist and noncommunist left—supported UNEF. François Longin, commenting on the demonstration in the progressive Catholic publication, *Temoignage Chrétien*, wrote:

> The government forbade this strike under the fallacious pretext that it would disturb the peace. So that the peace would not be disturbed it [the government] sealed off entire neighborhoods, closed métro stations, put Paris in a state of siege, and sent several injured people to the hospital.[62]

Soon even right-wing publications such as *Rivarol* and *Aspects de la France* (the latter continuing the tradition of the *Action française*), while not supporting UNEF, were making anti-Gaullist capital out of the state of higher education.

The demonstration received, however, little exposure over the government controlled Radio-Télévision Française. Three employees of the RTF were present at the demonstration and filmed the event, but television viewers were never to see these films. According to *Le Monde*, the Minister of Information, Alain Peyrefitte, directed the network not to show the films on the grounds that a demonstration in a section of Paris is not of sufficient importance to be televised nationally. *Le Monde* ironically commented by juxtaposing a broadcaster's brief mention of the demonstration on the 10 P.M. news program and the extensive coverage which this same newscaster devoted to a comedy film being made by Louis de Funès and to the search for the body of a woman believed to be drowned in the port of Boulogne-sur-Mer.[63]

UNEF also received support from a less expected source, the Conseil Général de la Seine. On the day of the demonstration the Conseil had voted its approval of the demands of the students and the professors. The minority Gaullist (UNR) group had refused to attend the session, the Préfet protesting that the issue was beyond the competence of the departmental body. When the Conseil defied the Préfet by unanimously voting to consider the issue, the Préfet and his officers had walked out of the session.[64] Support for the students and teachers had come from the conservative Center Republicans and Independents as well as from the left wing of the Conseil. When the Préfet left the meeting an Independent had cried out: "This is organized dictatorship!" [65] He and a Center Republican defended the contention of a communist representative that the demonstration was forbidden in order to provoke incidents which would discredit the student and professorial groups, and he commented: "After all, Boulevard St.-Michel belongs to the students and, if they demonstrate in the street, it is because they have no other place to go. . . ." [66]

Later in December the Administrative Council of the CNO decided to raise rents at the cités universitaires. UNEF protested and planned its second demonstration. The government banned this demonstration also; UNEF protested the ban and organized rent strikes at the cités universitaires. This tactic proved to be effective, for the government cancelled the increases.[67]

One of UNEF's demands during the "Week of Action" had been that the government discuss with UNEF the question of reforming higher education. The Minister appointed a commission of eighteen men to study the problem. At the end of January the Commission de Réforme de l'Enseignement Supérieur informed UNEF that it could submit its ideas on two mimeographed pages and that it would be granted thirty minutes to testify before the Commission on February 10. UNEF declined the invitation, reminding the Commission that it had already sent statements concerning its views to members of the Commission and maintaining that thirty minutes would hardly suffice to discuss a question of such complexity and importance. It accused the government of attempting to mislead the public into believing that students were being consulted, when in fact the government was not interested in their views.[68] An accommodation was subsequently reached whereby a delegation from UNEF would meet with the Commission on the 24th for a longer period of time. However, this was cancelled by the Minister during the course of the "Segni Affair."

After the "Week of Action," leaders of the AGE at Paris-Letters had entered into separate communication with the Minister, who agreed to attempt to alleviate some of the pressure on the Sorbonne by constructing classrooms in the Grand Palais and the Halle Aux

Cuirs by the next academic year (1964–1965). He refused, however, to discuss the other issues and other demands. The first of these was that students be accorded some representation on decision-making bodies at the Faculty. The second was that the government supply funds for the creation of a student directed center to provide free mimeographed copies of course lectures.[69] French students have become heavily dependent upon these mimeographed booklets, or *polycopiés*, which are quite expensive when purchased from an AGE or a commercial publishing house.

Receiving little satisfaction from the Minister, the leaders of Paris-Letters contacted leaders of seven other Parisian AGES, to plan a strike and demonstration in Paris on February 19.[70] At the request of the AGE in Paris-Law, the date was changed to the 21st. On the evening of the 13th the government announced that it planned to receive President Segni of Italy at the Sorbonne on the 21st. President Segni would be escorted by M. Fouchet. The leaders of Paris-Letters met with other Parisian leaders and successfully urged that they carry on with their plans. Of the original chapters involved only the majoritaire AGE of Paris-Science withdrew.

The National Bureau, which had played no role before the 13th, was apprehensive. The president, Michel Mousel, feared that if the leadership of Paris-Letters carried out the plans, it would result in a violent confrontation, "a massacre." And he feared that, in the eyes of both the public and the students, UNEF would be held responsible. In the March issue of UNEF's *21·27: l'Etudiant de France*, Gérard Poitou wrote: "It is certain that we were also afraid—afraid that the police, given the orders that they had, would provoke another Charonne." [71]

The Bureau found itself in a dilemma. There was nothing in the statutes of UNEF which gave the Bureau the right to order affiliated AGES to cancel strikes or demonstrations. The leaders at Paris-Letters were determined to see it through, and the National Bureau possessed little in the way of bargaining power. On the 13th the National Bureau decided that their only course was to make the demonstration of the 21st a nationwide one and to assert what control it could over the events. Relations between the national leaders and the leaders of Paris-Letters became strained.

On the morning of the 14th Mousel was called into the office of the Rector of the University of Paris. The Rector, Mousel claims, expressed sympathy with the student demands but warned that things would go very badly if demonstrations were to mar President Segni's visit. In the afternoon the National Bureau drafted a letter to the Minister of Education, requesting that the Minister express himself on the demands made in November. On the 15th, Mousel, anxious to have something which looked like a "victory" to strengthen his bargaining hand vis-à-vis the leaders of Paris-Letters, telephoned the Ministry. He was told that the Ministry would have no further contact with UNEF. Mousel believes this was a deliberate attempt by the government to push the National Bureau into taking extreme actions which would cost it the support of many members and alienate public opinion.

On the 18th Mousel made public a letter which he had sent to President Segni in care of the Italian Ambassador in Paris. The following is a translation of the complete document:

> Like all of their fellow countrymen, French students have appreciated your interest in the educational system of their country, an interest expressed by your intention to come to the Sorbonne and to attend the reception of the Council of the University of Paris.
>
> For us this is precious testimony of the reputation which French education has maintained in foreign countries. This is even more touching in the case of Italy, a country with which we have so many ties of affection and culture.
>
> The Union Nationale des Etudiants de France is, however, asking students to demonstrate during the day of your visit. It would be discourteous if we were not to explain to you the motives for this action.
>
> French education is in the midst of a very grave crisis. Ill-adapted in its spirit and methods to the conditions of [our] society, it is, moreover, deprived in catastrophic proportions of the material resources which would permit it to perform its task. In the course of the month of November 1963, professors and students tried to direct the attention of the public powers to this dramatic situation by a week of common action. The discussions which have since taken place between UNEF and the Ministry have yielded no results. It seems to us impossible to allow opinion to believe that we have ceased our action or abandoned our goals. This is why we must now

act again. In no case must this be interpreted as any sort of hostility directed toward you, Mr. President. The profound respect that we show for you, and, through you, for the Italian people, testifies to that.

We should like to have been able to welcome you, friend and representative of a great allied people, in a democratic university having the means to perform its functions. The circumstances prevent us from doing so. Our only desire is that you do not form a severe judgment of the sense of hospitality of French students. It is due to a simple sense of shame that they refuse to receive you in the ruins of what once was French education. It will not always be so.

Hoping that you will understand our embarrassment and our excuses, *je vous prie d'agréer, monsieur le président, l'assurance de mon plus profound respect.*[72]

At approximately the same time the leaders of the AGE at Paris-Letters sent an ultimatum to Premier Pompidou. The last three paragraphs of the letter read as follows:

> . . . we have learned that this date [the 21st] coincides with the visit of the President of the Italian Republic to the Sorbonne. Obviously, we do not wish to prohibit this visit which, in itself, does not concern us. But the fact that M. Segni will be accompanied to the Sorbonne by a member of the government has a very precise political significance for us.
>
> We should be treating the interests of those who entrusted us with their defense very lightly if, for any reason, we were to allow a member of the government to enter the Faculty unless . . . the above five demands [doubling of the number of *assistants*, tripling the number of class rooms, institution of a center of free *polycopiés* under student control, recognition of the *syndicat* as a participant in the decision-making process at the Faculty, opening of negotiations with UNEF over the institution of the *allocation d'études* in the near future] are met.
>
> We thus solemnly warn the government that the students of the Sorbonne will respect their commitments made in November and that, if they are disregarded, the government alone will bear the responsibility, before the students and public opinion, for the incidents caused solely by its educational policy.
>
> Consequently, the Fédération des groupes d'études de lettres is

maintaining its call for a strike and occupation of the Sorbonne on February 21, beginning at 1 P.M.[73]

On the 19th the Préfet of Police forbade the demonstration. He stated that his reasons for doing so were the same as his reasons for forbidding the demonstration of November. He went on, however, to accuse the students (he mentioned neither UNEF nor the AGE at Paris-Letters specifically) of intentionally planning the action to coincide with the Segni visit and thus of violating elementary rules of "decency and courtesy." [74]

On the same day another member of the power structure spoke out. This was *La Nation*, a publication of the Gaullist party and a constant critic of UNEF.

> In truth, for a long time now the politization of certain student movements (under the cover of syndicalism) has accustomed us to such outrages. . . .
> However, in the letter addressed yesterday to M. Segni, President of the Italian Republic, who is on an official visit to Paris, it would seem that M. Michel Mousel, President of UNEF, has exceeded the tolerable limits of the situation.
> That the president of a student association, in a letter made public, would try to discredit his own government in the eyes of a foreign chief of state (at the very hour when this chief of state has come to France to discuss not only problems concerning the fate of the two countries but, perhaps, of Europe), this, let it be said clearly, is inadmissible.[75]

In student quarters UNEF came under attack from the Action Etudiante Gaulliste, the Fédération des Etudiants de Paris, the Fédération Nationale des Associations d'Elèves en Grandes Ecoles, and the majoritaire AGE at Paris-Science.[76] The FNEF seems to have decided to hold its fire until the demonstration materialized.

On the 20th, UNEF, for the first time to our knowledge, found itself in open and direct conflict with the Rector and the deans of the five faculties of the University of Paris. The administrators released a short public statement:

> The Rector and the deans of the five faculties remind the students of the rules of hospitality which the University of Paris intends to

observe faithfully toward its guests. They judge to be inadmissible a project which imperils the dignity and the prestige of the University. They direct the attention of students to the gravity of the situation which a minority of them, unconscious of the responsibilities that it pretends to assume in the name of all, propose to create.[77]

As the 21st approached, the situation had been so confused by UNEF's internal factionalism that it was difficult for even the most constant sympathizers to support the organization. Paul Vignaux, the Secretary General of the Syndicat Général de l'Education Nationale (CFTC), was thoroughly alienated and withheld the support of the SGEN.[78] The columns of the always attentive and sympathetic Girod de l'Ain reflected uneasiness over the course of events. Discussing the letter of the student leaders of the Sorbonne to Premier Pompidou, Girod de l'Ain wrote:

> One can understand that the students, or at least an active minority, would want to see their demands realized. But to whom is this ultimatum addressed? To M. Fouchet for free *polycopiés*? Or to the teaching corps in order to gain representation on faculty assemblies? Or do they expect M. Segni to defend the cause of French education? [79]

The only open support from the outside was a qualified statement in favor of "diverse actions to make good the demands of UNEF" issued by the Syndicat National de l'Enseignement Supérieur, and a statement of solidarity by the secretary general of the association of students in letters of the National Union of Italian Students.[80]

At the Sorbonne the leaders of the AGE secretly passed the word that, instead of occupying the Sorbonne on the 21st, students should meet at 6 P.M. that very day, the 20th, to seize and hold the Sorbonne during the night. Only about 400 students responded to the call.[81] This lack of support gave the National Bureau an important advantage in dealing with the leaders at Paris-Letters.

The government delivered a final warning to UNEF, threatening to withhold their subsidy again and to rescind the organization's right to participate on the Administrative Council of the CNO as well as on other advisory committees, unless the demonstration were called off. It further warned UNEF's leaders that they would be open to prosecution on three criminal charges: harm to the security of the state, insult to a foreign chief of state, and the holding of a forbidden demonstration. And it informed UNEF that its delegation would not be permitted to testify on the 24th before the commission studying higher educational reform.[82]

The government also made a show of physical strength. Detectives searched the Sorbonne for students who might be hiding there. The Sorbonne and the Faculty of Science were then closed and guards were placed at the entrances. The ultimate attempt at dissuasion, however, was the force of approximately 5,000 policemen, mobile gendarmes, and officers of the CRS which took control of the Latin Quarter.[83]

On the afternoon of the 20th the National Bureau had announced that the demonstration would go on as scheduled. In the evening the leaders of Paris-Letters, disappointed by the poor response to their call for an occupation of the Sorbonne, met with the national officers. At midnight the National Bureau issued the following press release:

> The propaganda campaign conducted by the government during the last three days, to which a certain number of university authorities have lent themselves, is tending to convince public opinion that the demonstration for student demands, in fact, constitutes an act of hostility toward President Segni.
>
> UNEF has already expressed the profound respect which it has for the President of the Italian Republic. Nevertheless, in order to be unequivocal on this point, UNEF has, in full agreement with the President of the National Union of Italian Students, decided to organize no demonstration to coincide with President Segni's visit to the Sorbonne. It nevertheless regrets that the visit of President Segni will take place in a Latin Quarter emptied of its students and surrounded by police.
>
> . . . [if demonstrations were to take place], the deployment of an unprecedented force of police in the Latin Quarter would render the situation extremely grave and would provoke dramatic incidents. UNEF refuses to take responsibility for such events, in which students would be the principal victims.
>
> UNEF thus makes the following appeal:
> 1. All students must, at all cost, avoid incidents with the police and, in particular, must not respond to provocations by rushing the barriers in order to get to their courses.

2. The demonstration foreseen for Friday, February 21, at 4 P.M. is cancelled.

3. All students are invited to participate in a meeting at the Faculty of Science (Halle Aux Vins) at 4 P.M. They should get final instructions from their AGE's immediately before the meeting.

If the government were to oppose this meeting in an enclosed area, it would be proof that neither the visit of the Italian President nor the "maintenance of order" are the real reasons for the banning of student demonstrations.[84]

The government did seal off the Faculty of Science and the dean prohibited the meeting. When UNEF's militants went to their chapters to receive final instructions they were informed that, for the first time since the Algerian War, UNEF was going to demonstrate on the Right Bank. While the government had over 5,000 law enforcement officers deployed in the Latin Quarter, the National Bureau decided to air its grievances near the railroad stations of the Right Bank at an hour when workers would be catching commuter trains to the suburbs.

Le Monde estimates that approximately 3,000 students demonstrated near the stations.[85] They then descended southeast to the first, second, and ninth *arrondissements*, arms interlocked, chanting "Fouchet Démission!", "Liberté Syndicale!", "Polycopiés Gratuits!", and "Allocation d'Etudes!" On hand, as a gesture of solidarity, was the president of the National Union of Italian Students. There were sporadic outbursts of violence between students and police. The most serious of these occurred when the police attempted to disperse a group which was shouting hostile comments about Secretary of State Herzog outside of the High Commissariat of Youth and Sports.[86]

The immediate consequence of UNEF's incursion onto the Right Bank was that several students and three police officers were slightly hurt and 163 people were arrested, including a member of the National Bureau. One hundred and thirty-eight students, 21 of whom were foreigners, were held overnight. All received warnings. Four students were arraigned—two for violence against police officers and two for offenses against the Chief of State.[87] In keeping with the policy of harassing newsmen who attempt to cover student demonstrations, four newsmen were arrested—two

French journalists, one correspondent for Radio Monte-Carlo, and a correspondent of the Columbia Broadcasting Company. Their film was confiscated.[88]

One of those arrested for striking a police officer was a twenty-one-year-old student of economics, Christian Desobry. Desobry readily admitted that he had struck the officer. He didn't know why, he was generally a peaceful sort; but there he was in the demonstration, the officer's face became larger and larger, and he struck out.[89] Desobry was sentenced to eight days in jail.

This was changing the rules of the game. During previous demonstrations acts of violence had occurred between students and police officers. Students had been physically abused by the police while under arrest—especially during the Algerian War. Students had been held overnight in jail. But no member of UNEF had ever before been sentenced to jail for an act committed during a demonstration.[90] Desobry became a living symbol of the government's violation of individual and syndical liberties. UNEF undertook to protest the procedures used by the government in Desobry's case. It claimed that: he was allowed to communicate with neither his family nor his lawyers until minutes before his trial, and then only briefly; people under the age of thirty were prevented from entering the Palais de Justice during the afternoon of the trial by a large deployment of police; inside the Palais the public was not allowed on the floor on which the trial was conducted.[91]

The National Bureau issued a public statement in which it made several points. First, Desobry was involved in the situation because he responded to the call for demonstration issued by the Bureau. In marked contrast to its position in November, the Bureau accepted full responsibility for the demonstration and declared that any legal action should have been initiated only against the president or members of the National Bureau. Second, the Bureau asserted that no incident of this nature would have taken place if it had not been for the "brutal" intervention of the police. The Bureau asserted that it was the police, not the students, who initiated the violence.[92]

The statement went on to describe the general pattern of the government's attitude and behavior toward UNEF: refusal to communicate with UNEF, let alone grant its requests; banning its demonstrations; using the demonstrations as an excuse for employing violence to intimidate the students. The Bureau announced that it would not be intimidated by these coercive measures and would continue its campaign for university reforms and for a democratization of the educational system.[93]

The day after the police broke up the demonstrations on the Right Bank, the action of the government was condemned by the Union des Syndicats CFTC de la Région Parisienne and by the student affiliate of the Parti Socialiste Unifié. On the 26th, six days after the leaders of the AGE of Paris-Letters had succeeded in atttracting only 400 students to the courtyard of the Sorbonne, between 5,000 and 6,000 students gathered there in response to a call from the National Bureau, to demand Desobry's immediate release.[94] To express syndical solidarity there were representatives of the central offices of the FEN and their university and secondary affiliates, of the SGEN, and, despite the warning issued by the Rector of the University against participation by those outside the university community, of the CGT and the CFTC. Diverse groups affiliated with the Colloque de la Jeune Génération extended their support. Georges Depreux, Secretary General of the Parti Socialiste Unifié and a former Minister of Education, took the microphone to express the support of his party.[95] UNEF emerged from the Segni Affair with its external support intact.

The rally at the Sorbonne was peaceful. The National Bureau assumed responsibility for avoiding clashes between police and students by asking students to leave the courtyard gradually and, at all cost, to avoid confrontations with the police officers stationed around the Sorbonne. Such was not the case everywhere. AGE chapters throughout France held similar rallies to call for Desobry's release. In Lyon approximately 800 students left a rally in the courtyard of the Faculty of Letters in groups of 20, then returned to the university area, where they were dispersed by the police. They regrouped a second time before the offices of the AGE; its president was appealing to the students to disperse when several hundred helmeted police officers charged them from each end of the street. They beat students who attempted to escape through the AGE offices and hurled tear gas grenades through the windows of the student restaurant in which dinner was being served. Students attempting to flee the restaurant were beaten.[96]

The president of the AGE announced that a total of 30 students were injured. Fourteen of them suffered tear gas burns, and three required hospitalization. Two police officers were slightly hurt. Damage to the restaurant was estimated at approximately 5,000 N.F. (approximately $1,000).[97] Eight students were arrested. Five of them were charged with unlawful public assembly and participation in an unannounced demonstration; one female student was charged with contempt, another with violence against a police officer. The latter received a more lenient sentence than Desobry, a fine of 300 N.F. (about $60) and court expenses.[98] The behavior of the Lyonnais police and this conviction, coming on the heels of the behavior of the Parisian police on the 21st and the Desobry conviction, set off a wave of demonstrations for *liberté syndicale* by numerous AGES supported by many workers' unions.

At the beginning of April, UNEF held its 1964 Congress. In his report to the Congress, Michel Mousel referred to the Segni Affair as "the most serious crisis in the history of our movement." [99] As an attempt to secure UNEF's demands by direct action, it was an admitted failure.

On 20 November 1964, M. André Fanton, a Gaullist deputy who has shown greater animosity toward UNEF than any other parliamentarian, asked the Minister of Education if, in the light of UNEF's adherence to the International Union of Students and of their behavior during the visit of the President of Italy, he would define precisely the attitude he planned to adopt toward UNEF in the future. That November the Minister belatedly responded by characterizing the demonstration during the state visit as "indecent," and by presenting a position which gave M. Fanton "complete satisfaction":[100]

> Under these conditions the government can no longer aid an association which places the desires of certain leaders to play a political role before the defense of the moral and material interests of its members.
>   I should like to clarify my thoughts on this matter. I find it entirely legitimate, normal, and even desirable, in a sense, that young students should express political viewpoints with all the intensity that they think necessary. If they want to create political action groups, I see no problem. But the Ministry of Education cannot support—or oppose, for that matter—this action which is out of its domain. Its assistance is and will continue to be given, as in the past,

only to forms of activity which represent the corporate interests of students as a whole and not of groups, whatever they be, which have made politics their essential concern.

Thus, I have recently received delegations for bureaux of all the national student movements and I took a strong interest in these contacts. Even when these diverse movements—and I am not talking about UNEF here—were more or less politically oriented, they appeared to me . . . to possess a legitimate interest in both the important problems of education and in certain aspects of student life entirely worthy of consideration.

I want to maintain these contacts and I ask only to see UNEF practice the same policy as these other associations. But I am forced to state, in reading the declarations of certain leaders . . . or in listening to them, that this does not seem to be the case today.

I regret this even more because the Ministry of Education has rapidly and efficiently brought about construction this year . . . which will permit a satisfactory opening of the academic year. This effort will continue. But my present preoccupation remains the realization of a reform of considerable importance. The Assembly knows the general lines of this reform on which I am consulting the academic community, systematically and methodically. I should like each person, beginning with the students, to make his contribution without a partisan political spirit and with only the common interest in mind.

It is with this sole concern that I am now studying the problem of the subsidies and the financial situations of the diverse student movements. Those among these movements who talk the loudest know perfectly well that I could use . . . their financial difficulties, which are well known to me, to paralyze them and that I have never done this and do not want to do it.

Their leaders must know, moreover, that it is not in the political atmosphere which is inevitable in these surroundings that the relations between the Ministry of Education and the students can find a healthy basis. I am not sure that, by asking their political friends (I am not speaking here of M. Fanton) to intervene in the Assembly, they are acting wisely.[101]

Thus, after the Segni Affair UNEF found itself without access to the Ministry, without its subsidy, and without the possibility of taking to the streets to publicize its grievances. When the newly invested Bureau did call for a march from the Mutualité to the Sorbonne on 3 December 1964,[102] the Préfet forbade the march.

The Bureau sent a conciliatory letter to the Minister of Education asking him to intervene on its behalf with the Préfet and to reopen communication with UNEF.[103] The response of the government was the deployment of several thousand police officers and troops of the CRS, carrying rifles and machine guns, which surpassed all displays of force the previous year.[104] The march was cancelled.

As of this writing, over three years after the Segni Affair, UNEF still finds itself in the same frustrated position. It has suffered a severe decrease in membership; it has gone deeply into debt; and it has experienced disruptive conflict and disagreement over ideology and action. In fact it is capable of little more than occupying the offices on rue Soufflot and printing and distributing tracts.

NOTES

1. Michel de la Fournière and François Borella, *Le Syndicalisme étudiant* (Paris: Editions du Seuil, 1957), p. 49.
2. *Ibid.*, pp. 50–51.
3. *Ibid.*, pp. 56–59.
4. See Jacques A. Gau, "Le Régime de sécurité sociales des étudiants" (thesis prepared for the Doctorat at the Faculté de Droit et des Sciences Economiques de l'Université de Paris, 1960). There is no formal tie between UNEF and the administration of the insurance program, the Mutuelle Nationale des Etudiants de France. However, informal ties between leaders of UNEF and of the MNEF have been close in recent years. The Gaullist newspaper, *La Nation*, accused UNEF of taking over the MNEF in a series of articles in late March and early April 1964.
5. See de la Fournière and Borella, *op. cit.*, pp. 150–162, and Pierre Gaudez, *Les Etudiants* (Paris: Julliard, 1961), pp. 172–184.
6. De la Fournière and Borella, *op. cit.*, p. 134.
7. *Ibid.*, pp. 135–137.
8. *Journal Officiel, Lois et Décrets* (17 April 1955), p. 3831. The law also stipulated that one of the five representatives appointed by the student associations must be enrolled in a grande école. Grandes écoles are institutions of higher education which offer training unobtainable in the traditional faculties. Most of them offer technical or commercial courses of study.
9. Alain Chiffre, *Les Sources du syndicalisme depuis 1945* (Paris: UNEF Centre de Documentation, 1963), II, 320–322.
10. Jean Meynaud, *Nouvelles Etudes sur les groupes de pression en France*

(Paris: Cahiers de la Fondation Nationale des Sciences Politiques, Librairie Armand Colin, 1962), p. 327.

11. Chiffre, *op. cit.*, p. 320.

12. The best source on UNEF and the Algerian War is Chiffre, *op. cit.* See also Gaudez, *op. cit.*, pp. 144–172, and de la Fournière and Borella, *op. cit.*, pp. 130–150.

13. De la Fournière and Borella, *op. cit.*, p. 63.

14. Chiffre, *op. cit.*, p. 191.

15. *Ibid.* The Conseil d'Administration no longer exists.

16. *Ibid.*, pp. 192–193.

17. *Ibid.*, pp. 204–206.

18. *Ibid.* Chiffre maintains that the pressure came from Lacoste (SFIO and Minister for Algerian Affairs), Morice (a Radical of *Algérie française* sympathy) and Chabandelmas (Gaullist).

19. *Ibid.*, p. 216. The portion quoted actually reads: ". . . Je ne saurais admettre que le Président de l'Union Nationale des Etudiants de France vienne . . . me parler d'une carence. . . ."

20. *Ibid.*, p. 218.

21. For further information on purported mistreatment of Algerian students and violations of the sanctity of the Cité Universitaire in December 1958, see *Gangrene*, trans. Robert Silvers (New York: Lyle Stuart, 1960). Publication and circulation of this book have been banned by the Gaullists.

22. Chiffre, *op. cit.*, p. 226.

23. *Ibid.*, pp. 229–230, and Meynaud, *op. cit.*, pp. 214–215.

24. Chiffre, *op. cit.*, p. 215.

25. *Ibid.*, p. 245.

26. *Ibid.*, p. 246.

27. It was Jeanson's review of Camus' *L'Homme révolté* that touched off the famous Sartre-Camus debate in the pages of *Les Temps Modernes* in the summer of 1952.

28. Chiffre, *op. cit.*, p. 248.

29. *Ibid.*, pp. 249–250.

30. *Ibid.*, p. 254, and interview with Bernard Schreiner, president of UNEF, 19 July 1964.

31. Chiffre, *op. cit.*, p. 265.

32. *Ibid.*, p. 264.

33. *Ibid.*, p. 278.

34. *Ibid.*, pp. 277–278.

35. During the academic year 1957–1958 the minoritaire Bureau had added to the numerical strength of UNEF by negotiating the affiliation, with a certain reservation of autonomy, of the approximately 6,000-member Union des Grandes Ecoles.

36. Chiffre, *op. cit.*, pp. 285–288.

37. *Le Monde*, 21 November 1963, p. 9. The amount of the subsidy

(35,000 N.F.) and the number of seats on the Administrative Council of the CNO awarded to the FNEF were based upon its claim to represent 30,000 members. As the court ruled, no true claims of membership or representation could have been made before the FNEF had had a chance to sell its membership cards and present its candidates during the school year 1961–1962. Moreover, there is considerable evidence to suggest that the FNEF, with the knowledge of the government, has consistently exaggerated its membership figures. The data at the Documentation Center of the French Consulate in New York reveal that while the FNEF claimed to have 40,000 members in 1965, it had actually sold only 13,985 membership cards. It was by this time receiving a subsidy of 90,000 N.F. while UNEF's subsidy of 100,000 N.F. was still being withheld.

38. See p. 41.

39. Chiffre, *op. cit.*, p. 296. For an interesting treatment of the antifascist movement see Michel-Antoine Burnier, "Les Existentialistes français et la vie politique 1945–1962" (thesis submitted at the Institut d'Etudes Politiques in Paris, 1962), pp. 105–108. The thesis was published in book form by Gallimard in 1966.

40. Simone de Beauvoir, *La Force des choses* (Paris: Gallimard, 1963), p. 643. This work, especially Chapter 11, is extremely interesting in its presentation of both the details and the general flavor of this period of agitation.

41. The political parties had their own silent and solemn protest on February 12. Called by the SFIO, it was participated in by the Communist Party, the Radical Party, the Parti Socialiste Unifié, and the FNEF, according to Chiffre, *op. cit.*, p. 298.

42. On the Congresses of 1962 and 1963 consult: *Le Monde*, 21–26 April 1962; *Le Monde*, 9–19 April 1963; Marc Kravetz, "Naissance d'un syndicalisme étudiant," *Les Temps Modernes*, XIX, No. 213 (February 1964), 1447–1475; and Antoine Griset and Marc Kravetz, "De l'Algérie à la Réforme Fouchet: critique du syndicalisme étudiant," *Les Temps Modernes*, XX, No. 227 (April 1965), 1880–1902, and XX, No. 228 (May 1965), 2066–2089.

43. *Le Monde*, 27 November 1963, p. 24, 29 November 1963, p. 14, and 30 November 1963, p. 24. UNEF continued to participate on The Administrative Council until December 1966.

44. *Paris-Presse l'Intransigeant*, 8 November 1963, p. 1. The chant "Des Amphis! Pas de Cannons!" referred to the government's large military investment, especially the nuclear strike force program (see Chapter 4, p. 91, above). The author was an eyewitness observer to most of the events in Paris discussed here and in the remainder of the chapter.

45. *Ibid.*

46. *Ibid.*

47. The *agrégation* is the degree possessed by most teachers at the uni-

versity level and by approximately one-third of the teachers at the secondary level. The CAPES is the degree possessed by approximately two-thirds of French secondary schoolteachers. On the preparation of French teachers see W. R. Fraser, *Education and Society in Modern France* (London: Routledge and Kegan Paul, 1963), Chapter 4.

48. *Le Monde*, 22 November 1963, p. 24.
49. *Ibid.*
50. *Ibid.*
51. *Ibid.*
52. *Ibid.*
53. *Le Monde*, 26 November 1963, p. 18.
54. *Le Monde*, 27 November 1963, p. 24.
55. *Le Monde*, 29 November 1963, p. 14.
56. *Le Monde*, 30 November 1963, p. 10.
57. *Le Monde*, 27 November 1963, p. 24, and 29 November 1963, p. 24.
58. *Le Monde*, 30 November 1963, p. 24.
59. *Ibid.*
60. *Le Monde*, 3 December 1963, p. 9.
61. *Le Monde*, 8–9 December 1963, p. 14.
62. Cited in *Le Monde*, 8–9 December 1963, p. 14. In reality only the demonstration was forbidden, the strike was not. During the academic year 1964–1965 the Minister of Education announced that academics who engaged in strikes would have their salaries reduced in proportion to their days of nonperformance.
63. *Le Monde*, 1–2 December 1963, p. 11, and 5 December 1963, p. 15.
64. *Le Monde*, 1–2 December 1963, p. 11.
65. *Ibid.*
66. *Ibid.*
67. Michel Mousel, *Rapport Moral* of the president of UNEF, delivered before UNEF's Congress of 1964.
68. *Le Monde*, 25 January 1964, p. 8.
69. *Le Monde*, 18 February 1964, p. 16, and Gérard Poitou, "La Police, le pouvoir, et l'UNEF," *21·27: l'Etudiant de France*, No. 6 (March 1964), p. 43. (This magazine is published by UNEF.)
70. The other AGES involved at this early stage were those of medicine, pharmacy, cartel of the écoles normales préparations littéraires, artistiques, and scientifiques, higher technical education, law, and science. *Le Monde*, 21 February 1964, p. 1.
71. Information regarding the attitude of the National Bureau during the Segni Affair is based upon two lengthy interviews with Michel Mousel, his *Rapport Moral* delivered to the 1964 Congress, and Poitou, *op. cit.*, p. 44.
72. *Le Monde*, 21 February 1964, p. 2.
73. *Le Monde*, 19 February 1964, p. 8.
74. *Le Monde*, 21 February 1964, p. 2.

75. *Ibid.* Cited from Pierre Oudry, *La Nation*, 19 February 1964.

76. The Fédération des Etudiants de Paris is a loose grouping of Parisian AGES. It has always been under majoritaire control because all AGES, regardless of their size, enjoy the same voting power. There are many small majoritaire AGES in Paris.

77. *Le Monde*, 21 February 1964, p. 2.

78. Interview with Paul Vignaux, 3 July 1964.

79. *Le Monde*, 21 February 1964, p. 1.

80. *Ibid.*, p. 2.

81. *Le Monde*, 22 February 1964, p. 10.

82. *Ibid.* UNEF and the Union des Grandes Ecoles released to the press the report which they had planned to submit to the Commission. See *Le Monde*, 27 February 1964, p. 17. In September, UNEF issued a more detailed brochure, *Manifeste pour une réforme démocratique de l'enseignement supérieur.*

83. *Le Monde*, 22 February 1964, p. 10.

84. *Ibid.*

85. *Le Monde*, 23–24 February 1964, p. 15.

86. *Ibid.*

87. *Ibid.* Despite the fact that Chief of State de Gaulle is now a partisan political figure and the effective head of the government, the legislation of the Fourth Republic which provides for punishment of oral and written offenses against the Chief of State is still enforced. The definition of an "offense" is vague.

88. On 3 December 1963, police officers accosted and damaged the equipment of a newspaper photographer and a television cameraman during clashes between police and students in Toulouse. See *Le Monde*, 5 December 1963, p. 15. This writer was forbidden by a police officer to photograph the Sorbonne when it was surrounded by police cordons.

89. *Le Monde*, 25 February 1964, p. 8.

90. *Ibid.*

91. *Ibid.*

92. *Ibid.*

93. *Ibid.*

94. Five thousand is the estimate of *Le Monde*, 6,000 that of UNEF. In any case the area was filled to capacity and some students were turned away by the police. *Le Monde* carried an announcement of the meeting in a box placed in the center of its article on Desobry's trial. Although *Le Monde* officially took no position (Girod de l'Ain had been critical of both UNEF's and the government's behavior before and on the 21st, calling the result a draw), the announcement amounted to free advertising. See *Le Monde*, 25 February 1964, p. 8.

95. *Le Monde*, 26 February 1964, p. 8, and 27 February 1964, p. 17.

96. *Le Monde*, 27 February 1964, p. 17. At the time of their action, the police claimed that a grenade had been thrown at a police van from

an unidentified car. The AGE denied that any of its members were involved and *Le Monde* reported that investigators believed the grenade was thrown by members of "a student group on the extreme Right." This was undoubtedly a reference to the militant and violently anti-UNEF Fédération des Etudiants Nationalistes. However, in a press conference which he had called to discuss the subject, the Préfet of Lyon stated:

"Grenade or no grenade, the situation would have been the same once the street was improperly occupied and had to be retaken. Under the conditions, you know, *hélas*, that on both sides some lose control over their actions." *Le Monde*, 28 February 1964, p. 75.

It would, however, be difficult to portray the actions of the police as being completely spontaneous, since they left the university and then returned to launch a coordinated attack with riot-control equipment.

97. *Le Monde*, 27 February 1964, p. 17, and Gérard Poitou, *op. cit.*

98. *Le Monde*, 28 February 1964, p. 15, and 29 February 1964, p. 8.

99. Mousel, *op. cit.*

100. *Journal Officiel de la République Française, Débats Parliamentaire, Assemblée Nationale*, Saturday, 21 November 1964, pp. 5522–5525. During the Assembly session of 22 February 1964, the day after President Segni's visit, M. Fanton had submitted the same question in written form. In the written question M. Fanton had asserted that he felt UNEF's past behavior was incompatible with the receipt of funds from the government. He implied that he had urged the discontinuance of the subsidy even before UNEF decided to become a regular member of the International Union of Students and long before the demonstration during the visit of the Italian president. The Minister submitted no response to the written question. His statement in November, however, indicated a complete acceptance of M. Fanton's position. See the *Journal Officiel* for the Assemblée Nationale session of 22 February 1964, p. 327.

101. *Journal Officiel* for the Assemblée Nationale session of 21 November 1964, p. 5523. After the Minister of Education terminated his reply to M. Fanton, two deputies, M. Claude Delorme (Groupe Socialiste) and M. Fernand Depuy (Communist), were quick to indicate that they wished to be considered "friends of UNEF" and proceeded to engage Messrs. Fouchet and Fanton in debate over the position taken.

102. The march was to have taken place at the end of a meeting held in a hall of the Mutualité. Both the meeting and the march were part of a "National University Week." From 30 November through 5 December 1964, UNEF, the SGEN, the Syndicat National de l'Enseignement Supérieur, and the librarians and research workers of the FEN, conducted debates, press conferences, appeals to elected representatives, contacts with other voluntary groups, and rallies to articulate essentially the same demands which they had articulated one year before.

103. *Le Monde*, 4 December 1964, p. 24.
104. During the demonstrations of November 1963 and February 1964, the paramilitary CRS either remained in their vans and buses or left their weapons locked in the vehicles. The spectacle of heavily armed troops massed in the Latin Quarter had great impact upon the students.

Chapter 4

Factors Conducive to
Student Activism in
Postwar France

Student activism, or the manifestation by students of a desire to influence their academic and/or their political and social environment, does not appear with equal scope and intensity in all cultures or during all epochs within a single culture. The "boys will be boys" explanation does not account for the variations revealed by historical and cross-cultural research.

The scope and intensity of student activism is a function of specific environmental or systemic factors. For example, Clark Kerr has attributed the changing tone of campus life in the United States, from the apathy of the late 1940's and 1950's to the activism of the 1960's, to: the transition from relatively elitist to mass higher education; the impersonal atmosphere which accompanies this increase in the number of students; the generally permissive nature of the American family, school, and college; the development of a distinctive "student culture"; and such "explosive" political issues as civil rights and Vietnam. "Beyond these two issues lie others of great concern—control of the bomb, adjustment to the computer, accommodation to the mass corporation and government agency, and much else." [1]

Postwar France would rank high on any scale which might be constructed to measure student activism. In this chapter we shall examine those elements of the social, academic, and political environments of the French university student which have stimulated his activism.

Socio-Cultural Factors

All commentators on the French family seem to agree on one point: it is an unusually hierarchical and authoritarian social institution. While American parents tend to be permissive and to allow the child great initiative, French parents generally establish and enforce rigid norms. The father is the patriarch, not to be bothered with nonsense. The mother is closer to the children, is more easily confided in, but is thoroughly supportive of the father's role.

Jesse Pitts, limiting his discussion to the French bourgeois family, writes: "The child is allowed little initiative—officially. The proper forms of behavior, the *principes*, exist once and for all, and parents require perfect performance before the child is allowed to make his own decisions." [2] Rhoda Métraux quotes the reactions of two French respondents to the permissiveness of the American family. According to a young Frenchman, "Formation in indispensable. If the child were left to himself, one would be making a misfit. . . . Here [in the United States] boys of twelve express themselves better than do those of eighteen in France. That can be very dangerous, that bungles gifts,"[3] A young Frenchwoman, commenting on the human product of American permissiveness, stated: "That child has not received any moral basis for action from her parents. While [my] parents were always telling me what to do, at the same time they tried to develop my own judgment and good sense. This education is much better than giving complete liberty to children. . . ."[4]

According to Laurence Wylie, the fundamental difference between the life of French and American adolescents lies in the definition of limits: "The French adolescent is left in no doubt when questions arise concerning his role in the family. 'So long as you live in this house, you'll do what we tell you to do!' says the

French father in the normally regulated household." [5] Wylie also asserts that the dependence of the French adolescent upon his family is insured by the difficulty of acquiring independent finances. Any money which the adolescent earns is expected to be turned over to his parents for the use of the family.[6] While Pitts, who limits his discussion to the bourgeois family, asserts that the child begins to perceive possibilities for evasion and relief from parental authority after he reaches the age of six,[7] neither Métraux nor Wylie seems to perceive such possibilities in their discussions of the general culture.

The role of the family in determining the future of the child is also of greater importance in France than in the United States.

> The average French child (and his parents even more than he) has a clear idea of the limits within which his ambition may be fulfilled. He knows to what social and professional class he belongs. There is no doubt about his family's traditional political, religious, and even aesthetic ideals, and he has been placed by both family and teachers in a well-defined intellectual category. Each of these classifications implies certain limitations and expectations so far as the child's future is concerned. For the normal French child, then, this clear definition of expectations makes the problem of fulfilling his ideal self-image relatively simple. He has only to accept and to live up to what is expected of him.[8]

The authoritarianism of primary and secondary schools in France reinforces that of the family:

> In school, the French child gets more of what he has gotten at home. . . . The school experience reinforces . . . [his] attitudes toward authority and elaborates the ways in which a Frenchman will join with others in formal and informal organizations.
> In dealing with the teacher the child will meet a typical implementation of the doctrinaire-hierarchical tendencies in French culture. On the one hand the teacher uses magisterial methods exclusively: there are definite standards of excellence, standards of what a cultured Frenchman should know, how he should express himself. The teacher makes relatively few allowances for the interests and fantasies of youth. Typically, he ignores his students' needs as children. He often talks to pupils of eleven and twelve years old on a level which supposes an intellectual maturity that they are far from

having reached. On the other hand the teacher defines the world into a set of clearly delineated principles, and what he wants from the students is easily apprehended by them. In his relationships with students the teacher attempts to maintain aloofness and impartiality.[9]

Explaining the lack of class discussion in the lycée (secondary school), a French woman schoolteacher commented: "That is true, but then we in France had great men for our professors; just think, in my time we had in Paris the greatest names—nobody would have dared to contradict them, nobody would even think of doing it." [10] A young man who did think of doing it, much to his disadvantage, stated: "Actually, I myself was thrown out of a lycée after making a disobliging and impolite remark to the professor during a philosophy class. I contradicted him too crudely. . . ." [11] A Frenchwoman who taught a class of Americans made this comment about her pupils: "American children enjoy too much liberty and independence. A child should fear his elders, otherwise he has no respect and becomes wild. . . ." [12]

Wylie concludes: "The older a French adolescent is, the more he tires of paternal authority and the ever repeated phrase: 'So long as you live in this house. . . .' The effect is to strengthen his determination to become independent." [13]

It is therefore not surprising that by the time the young French person reaches university age he craves independence from hierarchical authority and the freedom to establish his own limits and, thus, his own identity. As we shall see, most male students leave their parents' households during the student years to live in private rented quarters or in university housing. In either case the young person views this change of educational status and residence as the liberating transitional point at which he becomes responsible for his own behavior. And the transition is marked by a ritual of rebellion. Because the commission of violence is viewed as a grave offense by the authoritarian family and school, French secondary school students traditionally celebrate success on the *baccalauréat* examination (which determines university acceptance) by creating a disturbance in the street and engaging the police in a good fight.[14]

The high degree of student activism in France is partially a collective reaction against the authoritarian process of socialization during childhood and adolescence. It is, however, a reaction which is not only accepted but encouraged and rewarded by the larger society. Young people, especially the students—from whose ranks will come the future political elites—are looked to as the hope for the nation's future. From Emile Zola to Michel Debré, prominent men in French political life have addressed their political writings to *la jeunesse.* Political parties exert great effort to recruit them. The press and the journals of literature and politics devote much more attention to student opinion and organizations in France than in the United States. Student leaders have been frequent contributors to major publications. Once a year *Le Monde* turns over its presses to UNEF for the preparation of a special edition with the *Le Monde* format and masthead. But there was a more impressive manifestation of how fully society accepted and encouraged the students' collective attempts to influence the decision-making process: the recognition and financing of UNEF as a public service association during the Third Republic and the investiture of students with important advisory, decision-making, and administrative responsibilities during the Fourth Republic.

Factors in the System of Higher Education

It is important to note at the outset that, unlike the United States, educational policy is centralized in the national government in France. Therefore, it is natural that student activists direct both positive demands and expressions of discontent to the government. Even if it were to devote its attention exclusively to corporate issues, a French student organization would have to be a "political" group.

The major premise of both the students in the Forces Unies de la Jeunesse Patriotique and the resistant professors who drew up the Langevin-Wallon Plan for the reform of the educational system was that a truly equalitarian society must be based upon an equalitarian educational system. The struggle against class bias in the recruitment of university students has been carried on by the minoritaires.

Tables 4–1 and 4–2 present data on the socio-professional standing of families from which university students are recruited.

TABLE 4–1 *Classification of Students in French Public Universities in 1961–1962 According to Faculty and the Socio-Professional Status of the Head of the Family (percentages)*

SOCIO-PROFESSIONAL CATEGORY OF THE FAMILY HEAD	FACULTY						THE CATEGORY AS PER CENT OF THE TOTAL ACTIVELY EMPLOYED POPULATION
	LAW	SCIENCE	LETTERS	MEDICINE	PHARMACY	TOTAL	
Farmers	4.8	6.2	6.3	4.1	4.8	5.7	15.7
Agricultural laborers	0.3	0.7	0.7	0.2	0.1	0.5	4.3
Owners of industrial and commercial concerns	17.8	17.6	17.5	20.1	24.2	18.2	10.4
Liberal professions and high administrative, management, and technical-scientific personnel	27.8	27.2	26.5	39.6	42.2	29.4	4.0
Middle administrative, management, and technical-scientific personnel and primary school teachers	15.9	17.9	24.2	14.2	13.0	18.8	7.8
Office workers and sales personnel	9.2	10.2	6.4	8.2	5.4	8.4	12.6
Workers	4.8	6.7	6.2	2.4	1.6	5.5	36.7
Service personnel	1.1	1.0	1.0	0.3	0.1	0.9	5.4
Other active categories	10.7	6.4	4.2	4.8	2.7	6.0	3.1
Inactive	7.6	6.1	7.0	6.1	5.9	6.6	—

SOURCE: The first six columns of figures are taken from the *Annuaire Statistique de la France 1963 (résultats de 1962)*, (Paris: Institut National de la Statistique et des Etudes Economiques, 1963), p. 57. The last column of figures was computed by the author from the data in *Tableaux de l'économie française 1963* (Paris: Institut National de la Statistique et des Etudes Economiques, 1963), pp. 122–123.

Table 4–1 indicates that, in 1961–1962, an educational advantage was acquired by those children whose families were in the upper socio-economic strata. The most glaring over-representation was of students from families in which the fathers were engaged in the liberal professions or held high administrative, management, or technical-scientific positions. Individuals in these categories comprised only 4 per cent of the actively employed population, yet sons and daughters of these individuals comprised 29.4 per cent of the university population. On the other hand, while industrial workers comprised 36.7 per cent of the actively employed popula-

TABLE 4–2 *Percentages of University Students from Working Class Families: Selected Countries* [1]

COUNTRY	YEAR	PERCENTAGE
United States	(early 1950's)	31.0
Great Britain	(1961–1962)	25.0
Norway	(1961)	25.0
Finland [2]	(1961)	17.6
Sweden [2]	(1960–1961)	14.3
Netherlands [3]	(1959–1960)	9.0
Austria	(1958–1959)	8.0
France	(1961–1962)	6.0

1. There is undoubtedly some slight variation in the occupational criteria used to define "working class" by statistical agencies in different countries. This table thus presents a comparison of the representation of children from what is considered to be the working class stratum *within* each national culture in the system of higher education.

2. For Finland and Sweden the percentages are of students entering upon their university careers in the specified years.

3. For the Netherlands the percentage is of male students only. Of the small minority of female students, from 3 to 5 per cent came from working class homes.

SOURCE: All but the French data are taken from: Richard F. Tomasson, "From Elitism to Egalitarianism in Swedish Education," *Sociology of Education,* XXXVIII, No. 3 (Spring 1965), 204–223. Courtesy of Richard Tomasson. The French figure is from *Annuaire statistique de la France 1963* (*résultats de 1962*) (Paris: Institut National de la Statistique et des Etudes Economiques, 1963), pp. 122–123. It represents only students registered in university *facultés.*

tion, their children comprised only 5.5 per cent of the student population.

The unequal representation is general, but the advantaged categories do enjoy greater advantage in the professional schools, especially in pharmacy and medicine, than they do in the faculties of science and letters. Students from working class families tend to gravitate toward the latter two faculties. When they do enter a professional faculty, it is most frequently law that is selected.

Table 4–2 presents comparative data on the recruitment of children from working class families into institutions of higher education in eight industrialized countries. The child of a working class family had a lower probability of entering an institution of higher education in France than in any of the other seven countries. This is despite the fact that the percentage of French students coming from industrial working class families had grown from 1.9 per cent in 1950–1951 to 5.5 per cent in 1960–1961.[15] In 1950–1951 American institutions of higher education were recruiting approximately 30 per cent of their students from working class families.

The campaign for more democratic recruitment is "corporate," in that it directly relates to the educational system. But inequalitarian recruitment has little immediate impact on the university student, for he has already been accepted into the system. For the average student, and thus for student politics, of much greater concern are the actual conditions under which he is forced to operate.

The brutal fact of university life in postwar France is that while the French university is constantly increasing its rate of recruitment among the eligible age group (Table 4–3), only one out of three entering students takes a degree. Thus France recruited 2 per cent more of its eligible age group into institutions of higher education than did West Germany and England in 1958–1959; however, its rate of attrition was so high that, in 1961–1962, Germany graduated the same percentage of the eligible age group as France while England graduated 2.6 per cent more than did France (Table 4–4). The four western European countries for which data are available show the following rates of attrition: France .66, West Germany .58, Sweden .50, England .20. The high French rate is even more shocking when one considers the strict routing procedures at the primary and secondary levels and the demanding nature of the *baccalauréat* examination.

TABLE 4–3 *Percentage of the Eligible Age Group Entering Institutions of Higher Education on a Full-time Basis: Selected Countries*

	1958–1959	1963–1964
France	9.0	13.8
U.S.A.	30.0	34.0
USSR [1]	5.0	7.3
Federal Republic of Germany [2]	7.0	7.3
Belgium	—	17.4
Sweden	12.0	—
England [3]	7.0	—

1. In the USSR the majority of students in institutions of higher education are part-time students. Thus while in 1963–1964, 7.3 per cent of the eligible age group entered such institutions on a full-time basis, 9.7 per cent entered them as part-time students. For France the percentage was 0.8.
2. The 7.3 figure for 1963–1964 includes 1.5 per cent of the eligible age group enrolled in teacher training institutes. In France, however, the institutions preparing primary schoolteachers, the écoles normales, are not considered to be institutions of higher education and the percentages for France do not include those enrolled in these institutions.
3. It is not specified whether the 7 per cent for England includes those enrolled in teacher training schools. In 1961, 2.5 per cent of the eligible age group entered teacher training schools. Six per cent of the eligible age group entered other types of institutions of higher education. The 1961 figures are for both England and Wales. It might also be added that, while 1958–1959 and 1963–1964 figures for Italy are not presented, it is reported that 6.0 per cent of the eligible age group entered Italian institutions of higher learning on a full-time basis in 1960. The percentage for the Netherlands in 1961 was 4.6.

SOURCE: The data are from Bertrand Girod de l'Ain, *La Réforme de l'enseignement supérieur* (Paris: *Le Monde*, 1964), p. 7, and Girod de l'Ain, "L'Enseignement dans neuf pars 'developpés,'" *Le Monde Sélection Hebdomadaire*, 10–16 March 1966, p. 7. The latter reports data gathered by M. Raymond Poignant for a forthcoming study to be published under the sponsorship of the Institut de la Communauté Européenne Pour les Etudes Universitaires.

This has caused widespread dissatisfaction. UNEF has attributed the phenomenon to four basic causes: insufficient academic and service facilities, insufficient programs of financial assistance, impersonal and authoritarian pedagogical conceptions, and poor post-

TABLE 4–4 *Percentage of the Eligible Age Group Which Entered Institutions of Higher Education in 1958–1959 Compared with the Percentage Which Actually Received Degrees in 1961–1962: Selected Countries* [1]

	PERCENTAGE ENTERING HIGHER EDUCATION ON A FULL-TIME BASIS IN 1958–1959	PERCENTAGE RECEIVING DEGREES IN 1961–1962
France	9.0	3.0
USSR	5.0	7.0 [2]
Federal Republic of Germany	7.0	3.0
England	7.0	5.6
Sweden	12.0	6.0

1. While it is not specified precisely, the percentage of those actually receiving degrees in 1961–1962 must be interpreted as referring to the number of those actually receiving degrees at the first university level over the total population of the age at which one *normally* receives the degree in the given country.

2. The percentage receiving degrees in 1961–1962 in the USSR can exceed the percentage of entering full-time students in 1958–1959 because of the high percentage of part-time students in that country. In 1963–1964, 9.7 per cent of the eligible population entered on a part-time basis while only 7.3 per cent entered on a full-time basis. The term "eligible age group" or "eligible population" can be quite misleading, especially in regard to part-time students. We must assume that both full- and part-time percentages were computed on the basis of the age at which students *normally* pass from secondary to higher education.

SOURCE: The data are from Bertrand Girod de l'Ain, *La Réforme de l'enseignement supérieur* (Paris: *Le Monde*, 1964), p. 7.

graduation employment opportunities. We shall consider these individually and at length.

From the beginning of the postwar period, the higher aspirations of the people and the programs of financial assistance for university students have resulted in a continual increase in the number of students. For a long time it had been apparent that in 1963–1964 the university would feel the full impact of the postwar baby boom. Yet, though it would be incorrect and unfair to maintain that nothing was done to anticipate this, it is evident that not enough was done. In a speech delivered to a meeting of the Inspection Générale at the beginning of the 1964–1965 academic year, Minister of Education Fouchet admitted: "For some time now the symptoms of a crisis in higher education have been visible." [16] Approximately 59,000 students passed the *baccalauréat* examination in 1960, and the Ministry estimated that it would have to deal with 145,000 successful candidates by 1969.[17]

Despite the magnitude of the problem, the expansion of educational facilities during the Fourth Economic Plan (1962–1965) fell 18.4 per cent below the goals set in 1961 on the recommendation of the Commission de l'Equipment.[18] Moreover, the government made it known that the expansion program in education was going to lag considerably behind the average for the combined ministries during the Fifth Plan. This provoked even the rigorously nonpartisan editors of *L'Année politique* to comment:

> Once again the Ministry of National Education is the victim of budgetary austerity, and a specially selected victim if one compares its 4.9 per cent rate of expansion in 1966 with the approximately 10 per cent rate of expansion which is the combined average for all of the ministries.
>
> One can only deplore the brutal cutback in the expansion of the budget of the Ministry of National Education, something which is absolutely incredible during a period of demographic expansion.[19]

This has meant, first of all, the serious overcrowding of academic facilities. The hardest hit of the academic districts was Paris, which accommodates approximately one-third of the total student population. The case of the Sorbonne, the home of the Faculty of Letters and the symbol of the French university, was notorious. During the academic year 1963–1964, many courses were over-enrolled and seats were on a first-come first-serve basis. Library facilities were so inadequate that most students simply did not use the library. Instead of going to class and reading in the library, many students read their books and mimeographed lecture notes in cafés. For the academic year 1964–1965 the government constructed more facilities in the suburb of Nanterre and, in response

TABLE 4–5   *Budgetary Appropriations Devoted to Education in France (1954–1966)*

YEAR	SIZE OF THE EDUCATION BUDGET (MILLIONS OF N.F.)[1]	EDUCATION BUDGET AS PERCENTAGE OF TOTAL BUDGET	RATE OF PERCENTAGE INCREASE OF EDUCATION BUDGET FROM PREVIOUS YEAR
1954	2,909	7.9	8.5
1955	3,237	8.2	11.3
1956	3,807	8.2	17.6
1957	4,531	8.0	19.0
1958	5,574	10.2	23.0
1959	6,581	11.0	18.2
1960	7,105	11.8	8.0
1961	8,499	12.7	19.6
1962	10,697	13.9	25.9
1963	12,760	14.1	19.3
1964	14,805	16.3	16.0
1965	16,457	16.8	11.2
1966	18,265	17.2	11.0

1. Before 1960 the education budget also included expenditures for cultural affairs which have since been allotted to a separate budget. These accounted for approximately 14 per cent of the total education budget. It must also be remembered that the figures in this column are not adjusted to take into consideration changes in the value of the franc.

SOURCE: *Annuaire Statistique de la France* (Paris: Institut National de la Statistique et des Etudes Economiques). (Percentages computed by the author.) The data for 1946 to 1964 are conveniently presented on p. 493 of the 1966 edition. The data for 1965 and 1966 are from p. 716 of the 1967 edition. These figures represent actual expenditures. Comparisons and analyses of initial budgetary appropriations in force at the beginning of each fiscal year are available in *Evolution comparée des budgets de l'Etat et de l'éducation nationale depuis 1900* (Ministère de l'Education Nationale, 1963), p. 19, and the 1963 through 1966 editions of *L'Année politique, économique, sociale, et diplomatique en France* (Paris: Presses Universitaires de France).

to the discontent manifested by students in 1963–1964, installed temporary classrooms in the Halle Aux Cuirs and the Grand Palais.

The construction of service facilities has also lagged because of the cutback in investment. The two most important service facilities are university housing and the student restaurants under the direction of the Comité National des Oeuvres. Rooms are provided at low rates (approximately $20 per month). The alternatives to living in university housing are living at home if one's family resides in the area, or renting private lodgings. Living at home reduces the student's feeling of independence. Living in private rented quarters is expensive, especially in Paris, where there is an acute housing shortage. The quarters that are reasonably priced are generally very dismal, very uncomfortable, and very poorly heated.

University housing facilities were able to accommodate only between 10 and 11 per cent of the student body in 1962–1963.[20] A survey of 455 students (conducted in 1961–1962 and 1962–1963) revealed that, of the male students, 14 per cent lived in university facilities, 34 per cent lived with their parents, and 52 per cent lived in private rented lodgings. Of the female students, 11 per cent lived in university facilities, 46 per cent lived with their parents, and 43 per cent lived in private rented lodgings.[21] In Paris 19 per cent of the students were accommodated in university facilities while 47.5 per cent lived with their parents and 33.5 per cent lived in private rented lodgings. In the provinces the corresponding percentages were 11.5, 35.5, and 53.0.[22] Under the Fourth Plan the government managed to construct 45,285 of the 52,000 new living places foreseen by the Plan.[23] Nevertheless, 83 per cent of the student body still either lived in the homes and under the control of their parents or found the means to rent private quarters.

Under the Fifth Plan the emphasis has shifted from the construction of cités universitaires—housing, restaurant, and recreational facilities independent of the academic facilities—to the construction of American-style campuses. While the importation of the concept of campus life makes sense in terms of available land, space priorities, and the growing university population, it has aroused a great deal of discontent among the students. The first problem is that French students generally like the urban atmosphere. A student living in a cité universitaire located in the outskirts or the suburbs of a city might spend his nights at the dormitory complex, but his days he spends in the city proper, where his academic facilities are located. The campuses, on the other hand, contain both living and academic facilities, and often have been constructed in outskirts or suburbs from which traveling into the city is inconvenient. Thus many students feel isolated from real life. In the words of one student, "the campus might be fine for American students, but it simply does not conform to the French spirit."

Even more important has been the consequent increase in regulation of student behavior. In 1963 and 1964, *in loco parentis* was simply not an issue for UNEF. In none of the five French housing complexes around Paris with which this writer was familiar were visits between the sexes barred. The policy of the American house at the Cité Universitaire Internationale, which forbade such visits under pain of immediate expulsion, was generally viewed as a puritanical idiosyncrasy of Americans. And while there was a general policy at the Cité Universitaire Internationale forbidding political activity in an effort to avoid importing international tensions, the Cité Universitaire in the Parisian suburb of Anthony was in a constant swirl of political activity. However, the construction of the campuses has been accompanied by the rigid application of rules forbidding both room visits between the sexes and political activity. This has led to a great deal of resentment in a milieu where the striving for independence is so intense.[24]

Another important service is the subsidized student restaurant. Every student in France is entitled to eat lunch and dinner in one of these restaurants for 1.30 N.F. (approximately 26 cents) without beverage. The government pays half the total cost of serving the meal, which is approximately 52 cents. The quality of the food varies of course with the individual restaurant and daily fortune; still, the student can eat a nutritious meal for approximately 30 cents, which is in Paris, where the cost of living is higher than in New York, an extremely important benefit.

Once again, however, the facilities are overloaded. In 1961–1962 there was a ratio of one restaurant place for every 6.2 students.[25] At the end of the Fourth Plan there was one place for every 5.7 students.[26] In most student restaurants in Paris, a fifteen-minute wait in line was normal, a twenty-five-minute wait not unexpected. The only really pleasant student restaurants are those in the cités universitaires, which are for the exclusive use of those fortunate enough to live there. Of course, waiting in line for a considerable time to eat in a crowded restaurant might not in itself pose an undue strain on students: however, as one of a whole complex of difficult working and living conditions, it eventually takes its toll.

A further problem for almost every student is the limited nature of the programs of direct financial assistance. There are at present four types of assistance available to students who meet the various criteria: scholarships (*bourses*), loans with little or no interest (*prêts d'honneur*), tax deductions for the family, and pregraduation contracts by which a student agrees to work for a public or private organization for a given number of years in return for the financing of his education.

UNEF reports that, in 1963–1964, only about 20 per cent of all students held scholarships and that, in 1964–1965, only 45 per cent of the students from working class families held them.[27] Pierre Gaudez estimates that the average stipend in 1960–1961 was approximately $32 per month (160 N.F.).[28] UNEF maintains that a study conducted at the University of Lille revealed that, when account was taken of the increased cost of living, the maximum scholarship for the preparation of the *licence* actually decreased in value by 13 per cent between 1958 and 1964.[29]

The result has been that students in the lower socio-economic brackets have been forced to rely heavily upon outside employment, and those in the higher brackets have had to continue being dependent on their parents. Table 4–6 presents the results of a survey conducted at the University of Lille by the Bureau Universitaire de Statistiques of the Ministry of Education. For no socio-economic group do scholarships account for even 25 per cent of the students' budgets. For the two lowest brackets the most important source of revenue is outside employment, for the higher it is the family; students in the middle categories are forced to rely heavily upon both.

It is indicative of the desire to assert independence from the family that even students coming from families in the two highest socio-economic categories derive between 20 and 25 per cent of their income from outside employment—approximately the same percentage that students from working class families derive from scholarships. UNEF maintains that, in 1963–1964, 40 per cent of

TABLE 4-6 Sources of Student Incomes by Socio-Professional Standing of the Head of the Family: the Academie of Lille (date unspecified, reported by UNEF in 1965). (In percentages of the income of all students in the given socio-professional category)

SOURCES OF INCOME	LIBERAL PROF., HIGH ADMIN., MGT., & TECH. & SCI. PERSONNEL	OWNERS OF INDUST. & LARGE COMM. CONCERNS	MIDDLE ADMIN., MGT., TECH. & SCI. PERSONNEL & PRIMARY SCHOOL TEACHERS	ARTISANS & SMALL BUS.	OFFICE WORKERS & SALES PERSONNEL	FARMERS & AG. LABORERS	SERVICE PERSONNEL & MISC.	WORKERS
Assistance from the family	66.1	66.8	46.8	46.7	34.0	45.3	26.7	24.5
Scholarships	7.3	6.6	14.0	13.8	22.0	15.1	23.4	23.6
Apprenticeships and pregraduation contracts	4.1	3.2	7.5	5.7	4.9	4.5	6.9	6.5
Outside employment	22.3	23.2	31.3	33.3	38.4	34.7	43.0	45.0
Other	0.2	0.2	0.4	0.5	0.7	0.4	—	0.4
TOTAL	100	100	100	100	100	100	100	100

SOURCE: L'Union Nationale des Etudiants de France, *L'Allocation d'études* (Paris, 1965), p. 4. Attributed to the Bureau Universi-

the students in France worked on a regular basis and 15 per cent had no source of income other than remuneration from outside employment.[30] François Mareschal, internal vice-president of UNEF in 1963–1964, expressed what he saw as the resulting dilemma of the French student in two equations: "family = assistance = dependence" and "moonlighting = salary = academic failure." [31]

Since 1950 UNEF has called and fought for a program of sustaining scholarships for all students (the *allocation d'études*).[32] It maintains that such a program is an absolute necessity if recruitment to the university is to be made more equalitarian, if the high rate of attrition is to be reduced, and if students are to attain the degree of independence due to young adults engaged in intellectual work. On this issue UNEF has considerable support within the student body. During the second semester of the academic year 1961–1962, a nonrandom sampling of almost 800 Parisian students revealed that 68 per cent favored the proposal while only 32 per cent were against it.[33] And although only 52 per cent of a random sample of students surveyed at the Faculty of Letters at Lille in 1963–1964 felt that student organizations should deal with "political problems," 92 per cent of the same sample agreed with the following statement: "A salary would give the student material independence and would preserve his personal dignity, both of which are necessary for his intellectual development." [34]

The major student opposition to the proposal comes from UNEF's rival, the Fédération Nationale des Etudiants de France. A tract distributed by the local FNEF organization at the Faculty of Law in Paris attacks the proposal as being "Marxist" and "utopian." It claims that it is "socially unacceptable because it is a prelude to the *fonctionnarisation* [transformation into government employees] of students, it accentuates the inequalities which it pretends to eliminate, it is designed to weaken family ties, and it makes the student a young intellectual worker in a family without classes." [35] The most interesting aspect of the criticism is the disapproving reference to the weakening of family ties, which seems an attitude shared by only a small minority of students. The FNEF, however, does agree that the present scholarship system is inadequate. It proposes an alternative system, of scholarships for all students working for higher degrees and improved scholarships and loans, based upon need, for students preparing the *licence*.

Another major source of student discontent is that the pedagogy of French university professors is impersonal and authoritarian, much more so than that of American professors. Almost no importance is attached to communication between students and professors at the level of the *licence*. The university student finds the same attitude of pedagogical infallibility and aloofness in the university classroom that he experienced in secondary school.

Teaching is done almost always in a large lecture course (*cours magistral*). The ratio of students to teachers in 1965–1966 was 7.5:1 in Great Britain, 8:1 in the USSR (for full-time students), 10:1 in the German Federal Republic, 13:1 in the United States, and 22:1 in France and Italy.[36] And this actually represented considerable improvement over the 1961–1962 French ratio, which was 27:1.[37] The success or failure of the student is determined entirely by his performance in a highly impersonal examination system. If a student has difficulty with material, he usually has no choice but to work it out by himself or with his friends, for professorial tutelage is almost nonexistent.

UNEF seeks a university which is democratic in both its recruitment and its teaching methods. This requires change both in basic pedagogical conceptions and in the structure of the university, as well as the employment of more teachers. UNEF is asking for the sparing use of the large lecture course and a heavier reliance upon learning situations in which students could play a more active, independent role and in which a two way flow between students and professors could be the norm. Most students feel that the present system of preparing university teachers, the *agrégation*, perpetuates the authoritarian perspective of teachers;[38] UNEF therefore calls for its abolition and for the establishment of institutes of pedagogy in which future professors would be required to take courses.[39]

UNEF also claims that the present French university is not able meaningfully or even adequately to prepare young people because its organization, substantially unchanged since the Napoleonic era, is based upon an archaic conception of academic disciplines. In order to improve research and teaching, it is necessary to abolish the traditional system of faculties and grandes écoles and to institute academic divisions and departments based upon the more modern conception of general areas of study and specific disciplines within the areas.[40] The influence of the American system, in which great interest is displayed by the French, is evident.

When UNEF calls for greater governmental investment in education, it enjoys the full support of the teachers' unions. When it touches upon questions of pedagogy and structure, however, even the most politically progressive professors react in a conservative manner. The academics have also been unreceptive to UNEF's requests for representation on faculty assemblies. UNEF's hope is that the younger academics—who have experienced the postwar university as students, and some of them as active syndicalists—will ally themselves with the students in urging these basic pedagogical and structural changes.

The fourth major source of student discontent and discouragement is perhaps the most serious in its long-term implications. Although the French university actually awards degrees to only 3 per cent of the eligible youths, making it thus an extremely elitist system, nevertheless, many of the graduates are unable to find satisfactory employment (*débouchés*). As indicated in Chapter 2, the problem of unemployment of intellectuals was so acute between the two world wars that university graduates were frequently retrained in manual skills. This situation was brought about by the severe economic dislocations of the period and the increased number of people entering institutions of higher education. The similarly heavy influx of students into faculties of letters in the 1960's—a number which is swollen by the entrance of students from working class families—has created a similar problem. In 1960 there were 52,000 students in letters and 74,000 in science. In 1966 there were 147,000 in letters and 122,000 in science.[41]

Students in the faculties of letters generally look forward to employment in the public sector. In a survey conducted at Aix-en-Provence in 1957, 72.5 per cent of the student sample in the Faculty of Letters expressed a preference for work in the public sector, 11.5 per cent for the private sector.[42] The major employer in the public sector is the Ministry of Education. It cannot, however, absorb all of the graduates, and there are not many alternative careers for people with *licences* in the humanities and social sciences.

In 1966–1967 fewer than one-third of the holders of the *licence* in history and geography could be employed as regular teachers. Yet, of the 275 students who had taken *licences* in history and geography at the Faculty of Letters of the University of Besançon since 1955, only thirteen were engaged in nonteaching careers as of March 1967, and eight of these were doing administrative work for the Ministry of Education. Most of the graduates could be employed only as temporary teachers and substitutes. As the dean of the Faculty stated: "There is a monstrous disequilibrium between the number of our students and the jobs which are available to them." [43]

Unemployment is a more severe problem for students in letters than in science. But in some areas, particularly mathematics and biology, even students with science degrees have considerable difficulty securing employment. A teacher in the mathematics program at the Faculty of Science in Paris reported to this writer that, of the approximately 1,600 students who anticipated taking a degree in the program in 1968, only approximately 200, or one-eighth, had found employment as of June.

The cumulative effect of difficult working and living conditions, authoritarian and impersonal pedagogy, a high rate of attrition, and the severe unemployment problem, which even the successful student faces, is twofold. First, to think of a career and the future is discouraging for a large segment of the student population. Because the future is so uncertain and the perceived difficulties of the present so gallingly certain, the attention of the student is directed to his present condition and his role as student. There is a high degree of solidarity with fellow students who find themselves in the same unpleasant situation. In countries where these difficulties do not obtain, or obtain to a significantly lesser extent, young people are more likely to view the role of student simply as a necessary transitional stage to a chosen occupation or profession. What solidarity does exist is more likely to be based upon common anticipations of future occupations.

Second, the inability of the economic and educational systems to absorb university graduates and the conviction that the government is completely insensitive to student problems have encouraged many young people to question the soundness of educational, economic, and political institutions and to think in terms of radical social change.[44]

As indicated in Chapter 3, the question of reforming higher education was studied throughout the academic year 1963–1964. Because of its confrontation with the government, UNEF was not allowed to testify before the commission studying the problem. The reforms which were enacted, the Fouchet Reforms, encountered strong objections from UNEF. They called for the degree programs in faculties of letters and science to be divided into three two-year stages, and the *licence* to be awarded after the first year of the second stage. Since the year of pre-Faculté preparation (*propédeutique*) was eliminated, the education of the holder of the *licence* was reduced by one year. Moreover, the best students completing the first stage of the program can now work directly for a new higher degree, the *maîtrise*, without taking the *licence*.[45] UNEF, most of whose members were working for the *licence* in letters or science, objected that the degree was being reduced to the status of a consolation prize. It charged that the reforms offered no basic solutions to the pressing problems of higher education. It accused the government of being interested only in supplying the technocratic-capitalistic system with a regular supply of personnel at the least possible cost and in the least amount of time.[46]

Factors in the Political Environment

World War II had a heavy impact on the tone and temper of university life in both France and the United States. In the United States the social base of recruitment was broadened when veterans took advantage of the free educations offered them under the G.I. Bill. The nation had stood relatively undivided in its feelings about the war and remained completely untouched by its destructiveness. The major interest of the veterans was to get an education and enter a secure professional life as quickly as possible. Political problems did not make much impact on the determined, career-oriented students of the late 1940's. Indeed, the immediate effect of the most important American political concern of the early and mid–1950's, McCarthyism, was to discourage political activism among all but the most right-wing campus elements.

The situation was different in France. Physically, the country had been heavily damaged by the war. Politically and morally it had been divided. Frenchmen had fought and killed their brother Frenchmen. Frenchmen had delivered other Frenchmen, especially French Jews, into the hands of the Nazis for torture, forced labor, and extermination. And Frenchmen had sent young Frenchmen, regardless of their religion or political activities, into forced labor in the service of the Nazi state. France had been literally two nations at war with each other. One nation, the resistors, emerged triumphant over the collaborators. The Liberation had become a time of moral revaluation for some and of settling scores for others. It was in this atmosphere that the attempt to turn UNEF into a student- and environment-oriented organization was undertaken by students who had been involved in the Forces Unies de la Jeunesse Patriotique. At a crucial point in French history, they maintained, UNEF had not met its moral and political responsibilities, and the students had been dishonored.

It would be difficult to overestimate the importance of the Resistance experience to the minoritaires. It was a lesson in morality and citizenship. As late as the end of 1957, Michel de la Fournière and François Borella dedicated their book to "the French students killed in the Resistance, who showed the young generations where the truth is and where their duty lies in time of peace as well as in time of war." [47]

The Liberation had also been a period of hope. Naziism and Fascism had been defeated. The collaborators and those who had remained silent were shown the errors of their ways. A new national and international order, based upon peace and social justice, was about to be created. As the preamble of the Charter of Grenoble states:

> The representatives of the students of France . . . conscious of the historic significance of an epoch,
>> In which the French Union is elaborating a new declaration of the Rights of Man and the Citizen;
>> In which a peaceful order among nations is being established;

In which the world of labor and youth is establishing the bases of an economic and social revolution for the benefit of mankind;
Affirm their will to participate in the unanimous effort of reconstruction.

The experience of World War II and the Liberation served to reinforce a very basic aspect of French political culture. Gabriel Almond has written:

. . . French political culture is not a homogeneous, fusional culture . . . rational components are distributed in different proportions in the society. The rational part of the culture takes the form of an absolute-value rationality rather than a bargaining, instrumental rationality. Its rationality tends to be apocalyptic rather than civic or pragmatic; and this has been as true of French Catholic intellectuals as it has been true of French Radicals, Socialists, and Communists.[48]

Almond contrasts this with the homogeneous, fusional (reconciling traditional and modern elements), bargaining, and instrumental political cultures of the United States and Great Britain.

Much of the "absolute-value rationality" of French political culture is due to the traditional role played by the intellectual in French political life. The noun, "intellectuel," first entered the French language during the Dreyfus Affair. There is some confusion as to whether the word was first used by the Dreyfusards with a sense of pride or by the anti-Dreyfusards with a sense of derision. Regardless of who coined the term, it was first employed denotatively to designate those people in the educational and literary world whose names appeared in *L'Aurore* to protest the unjust treatment of the Jewish officer at his second military trial.[49] The victory of the Dreyfusards reinforced the tendency of Frenchmen of thought and letters, especially those in the academic community, to feel a special responsibility in the civic domain. Learned and contemplative, remaining outside the seat of power and above considerations of personal loss or gain, they have assumed the role of spiritual guardians of the secular state. Their examplars are Socrates, Voltaire, and Zola. Their scripture is Julian Benda's *La Trahison des clercs.*[50]

The students who drafted and ratified the Charter of Grenoble

announced to the nation that they considered themselves intellectuals and that, as such, they had the duty "to seek, propagate, and
defend the Truth, which implies the duty to spread and further
cultural life and to interpret the direction of the course of history;
to defend liberty against all oppression, which is, for the intellectual,
the most sacred mission."

UNEF's leaders made no secret of their general disgust with
Gaullism after the confrontations of 1963–1964. Their *Manifeste
pour une réforme démocratique de l'enseignement supérieur* of
September 1964 indicted Gaullism for its technocratic capitalism
and marked the beginning of an openly anti-regimist campaign.
Before that time, however, the official noncorporate positions taken
by the minoritaires had been limited to specific developments in
the international environment and/or to the French posture therein.

This interest in issues having international implications derives
from several factors. First, France had recently been ravaged in a
world war and occupied by a foreign power. Second, the continuation of the colonial policy and the prosecution of wars against
national liberation movements by postwar French governments
seemed to contradict the equalitarian and libertarian principles of
the struggle against Naziism and Fascism. Their war experience
and ideals had sensitized the students to the perspectives and problems of the colonized, the emerging nations. Third, there was an
absence of any single domestic issue with the explosive impact
which the race issue has had in the United States. The issue of
the adoption of a new constitution and the installation of the
Gaullist regime was directly related to the Algerian problem and,
in the minds of the minoritaires, subservient to it. Fourth, the
continuing international conflict and cleavage, the cold war, has
had a more immediate and weighty impact upon students in France
than in the United States or in other Western European countries,
with the possible exception of Italy. This is because French political
culture is internally divided over the same ideological issues which
are being contested in the international arena. The cold war has
been important in the persistence of an ideologically diverse and
intense political culture in France.

Minoritaire policies and pronouncements on noncorporate issues
have been of three general types: condemnation of acts or policies
which seemed unjust and oppressive, and expressions of support

for the victims; opposition to the creation of a French nuclear strike force; and maintenance of relations with both the International Union of Students and the International Student Conference.

Delegations from numerous foreign student organizations attend UNEF's congresses, many of them to seek support for a particular cause or condemnation of a particular policy.[51] Some of the more notable objects of condemnation have been: continued French colonialism (after 1962, in Guiana, Gaudeloupe, Martinique, and Réunion); Portuguese colonialism and wars against insurgents in Mozambique and Angola; racism in South Africa; anti-Semitism in the Soviet Union; Soviet intervention in Hungary; American intervention in Vietnam; and the attempt to suppress nonregimist student- and environment-oriented organizations in Spain and Morocco.

UNEF has also opposed the creation of a French nuclear strike force. This opposition is based partially on a concern that the proliferation of nuclear weapons poses a threat to peace, but also upon the feeling that the educational system is being deprived of needed financing because of the size of the defense budget.[52] To protest what they regarded as false priorities, student demonstrators chanted "classrooms, not guns!" and UNEF became affiliated with the largely symbolic and inactive Comité National Contre la Force de Frappe.

As an attempt to bridge cold war barriers at the student level, UNEF has been the only student union from a western nation to maintain simultaneous relations with the communist-dominated International Union of Students and the western-oriented International Student Conference. Since the formation of the ISC in 1950, there have been three distinct periods in UNEF's relations with the two opposed organizations. From 1950 to 1956, when UNEF was under majoritaire control, it had no relations with the IUS but was a regular member of the ISC. From 1956, when the minoritaires came to power, to 1962, UNEF belonged to the ISC and only observed the meetings of the IUS. From 1962 to 1966 UNEF became progressively estranged from the ISC while developing a closer relationship with the IUS.

During the summer of 1962, UNEF's delegation joined those student organizations from Yugoslavia and twenty-five emerging nations in walking out of the meetings of the ISC, after the latter had refused to seat a delegation from Puerto Rico as representatives of a national union. The refusal of the ISC to condemn American policy in Vietnam further alienated the minoritaires.[53] In the summer of 1964 the ISC adopted a new charter, which UNEF refused to ratify.[54] However, in 1966 UNEF accepted "associate member" status in the ISC, which did not require ratification of the charter and permitted UNEF to participate in the debates without possessing the right to vote. The recent revelations of the relationship between the ISC and the CIA leave the future of the ISC, much less UNEF's role in it, very much in doubt.[55]

Closer relations with the IUS were initiated in the summer of 1963, when UNEF was still a regular member of the ISC. At the General Assembly of July, the National Bureau argued that such relations were necessary if UNEF was to maintain contact with the many student unions from the developing areas which affiliated only with the IUS. This was a serious concern, because many of the unions which had walked out of the 1962 meetings of the ISC made it known that they had no intention of returning. Therefore UNEF's General Assembly voted to adopt the status of "associate member" in the IUS, as later they would in the ISC. In this instance associate membership meant that UNEF possessed the right to participate and to vote at the meetings of the IUS without themselves being bound by the decisions.[56] Approximately nine months later UNEF's 1964 Congress voted to adopt the status of a regular member in the IUS.

The minoritaires' policy of dual affiliation has permitted UNEF: to maintain contacts with students from countries on both sides in the cold war; to develop closer ties with the many student associations from the developing nations which affiliate with one or the other international environment-oriented organizations; to present an image of relative objectivity on the issues which divide the international student world; and to placate both communist and noncommunist activists within its own ranks. It is ironic, in the face of M. Fanton's attack upon UNEF for its relations with the IUS,[57] that the foreign policy posture adopted by the Gaullists in the mid–1960's bears a striking similarity to the role UNEF has played in international student circles since 1956.

How can UNEF take a position between an IUS which presents, in its procedures and its organization, every appearance of "democratic centralism," and an ISC which embraces the hypocrisy of the defenders of "freedom"? Isolation is not tenable. It is neither moral (because colonialism still survives in the world) nor effective (the national unions of the developing areas are pressing us to take positions on their problems and, if we want to open the way to fruitful cooperation with them, the best path is certainly not that of aloofness). The solution adopted by UNEF is very pragmatic.[58]

NOTES

1. Clark Kerr, "From Apathy to Confrontation" (address delivered before the Conference on Students and Politics, San Juan, Puerto Rico, 25 March 1967).
2. Jesse R. Pitts, "Continuity and Change in Bourgeois France," in Stanley Hoffman et al., eds., *In Search of France* (Cambridge: Harvard University Press, 1963), p. 250.
3. Rhoda Métraux, "Themes in French Culture," in Rhoda Métraux and Margaret Mead, *Themes in French Culture: A Preface to a Study of French Community* (Stanford: Stanford University Press, 1954), p. 31.
4. *Ibid.*
5. Laurence Wylie, "Youth in France and the United States," in Erik H. Erickson, ed., *The Challenge of Youth* (Garden City: Anchor Books, 1965), p. 291.
6. *Ibid.*, p. 305.
7. Pitts, *op. cit.*, p. 250.
8. Wylie, *op. cit.*, p. 298.
9. Pitts, *op. cit.*, pp. 254–255.
10. Métraux, *op. cit.*, p. 42.
11. *Ibid.*, pp. 42–43.
12. *Ibid.*, p. 31.
13. Wylie, *op. cit.*, p. 305.
14. Métraux, *op. cit.*, p. 8.
15. Conseil Français des Mouvements de Jeunesse, *Présence de la jeunesse* (Paris: Privat, 1955), p. 29. The representation of students from families of agricultural workers fell from 0.9 per cent of the total student body in 1950–1951 to 0.5 per cent in 1961–1962. We do not know what percentage of the total active population was represented by agricultural workers in 1950–1951. For an extended treatment of the problem of class representation see P. Bourdieu and J. C. Passeron, *Les Héritiers: les étudiants et la culture* (Paris: Editions de Minuit, 1964).

16. Speech of 1 October 1964.
17. Bertrand Girod de l'Ain, *La Réforme de l'enseignement supérieur* (Paris: *Le Monde*, 1964), p. 5.
18. *L'Année politique, économique, sociale, et diplomatique en France 1965* (Paris: Presses Universitaires de France, 1966), p. 397.
19. *Ibid.*, pp. 405–406. The expression "rate of expansion," as used by the editors of *L'Année politique*, refers only to the increase in expenditures for new programs of construction and expansion of facilities (*dépenses d'équipment—autorisations de programme*). The percentages in the fourth column of Table 4–5 include increases in appropriations for normal operations (*dépenses de fonctionnement*) and increases in appropriations for expansion programs authorized in previous years (*dépenses d'équipement—crédits de paiement*) as well as increases for newly authorized programs of expansion. In 1966 the increases over the previous year in funds devoted to normal operations and to previously authorized programs of expansion were, respectively, 12.1 and 6.2 per cent.
20. *Ibid.*, pp. 398–400. Computed by author. Also see *Education in France*, No. 28 (June 1965), p. 8.
21. Pierre Bourdieu and Jean-Claude Passeron, *Les Etudiants et leurs études* (Paris: Mouton, 1964), p. 25. Almost all the students in the sample were drawn from the faculties of letters at the Universities of Bordeaux, Lille, Lyon, Paris, Rennes-Nantes, and Toulouse. They were studying psychology, sociology, or philosophy.
22. *Ibid.*, p. 36.
23. *L'Année politique, économique, sociale, et diplomatique en France 1965, op. cit.*, p. 400.
24. The attempt to enforce these rules at the Nanterre campus was an important part of the catalytic process leading up to the student revolt in May and June 1968. It is interesting to note that the residents at the American house at the Cité Universitaire Internationale also revolted during the crisis and won the right to visit the rooms of members of the opposite sex.
25. *L'Année politique, économique, sociale, et diplomatique en France 1965, op. cit.*, p. 400. Computed by the author. As in the computations of the percentage of students in university housing, the base includes only those students registered in the faculties and the public grandes écoles.
26. *Ibid.*, pp. 398–400.
27. *L'Allocation d'études*, (Paris: Cahiers de l'UNEF, No. 8, 1965), pp. 6 and 8. In 1966–1967, approximately 19 per cent of the students held scholarships. Florence Ribon, *Condition des étudiants* (Paris: Tendences, No. 47, June 1967), p. 22.
28. Pierre Gaudez, *Les Etudiants* (Paris: Julliard, 1961), p. 41.
29. *L'Allocation d'études, op. cit.*, p. 6. The amount of French scholarships

is extremely variable. After the 10 per cent cost of living increases granted in September 1960, the minimum stipend for a student working for the *licence* was 720 N.F. (approximately $144) per year and the maximum stipend was 2,880 N.F. (approximately $576) per year. Information courtesy of the Documentation Center of the French Consulate in New York.

30. *Ibid.*, p. 5, and *Manifeste pour une réforme démocratique de l'enseignement supérieur* (Paris: Cahiers de l'UNEF, No. 7, 1964), p. 21. Also see Bourdieu and Passeron, *op. cit.*, pp. 10, 25. In their 1961–1962 and 1962–1963 survey of 455 students, Bourdieu and Passeron found that 31 per cent of the males and 22 per cent of the females were employed and that students who work devote less time to their studies than do students who do not work. They make no distinction between regular and irregular employment. For an excellent and more recent discussion of the living conditions and financial situation of French students see Ribon, *op. cit.*, p. 24. Ribon maintains that, during the academic year 1966–1967, 33 per cent of the students worked during the entire year while 25 per cent worked only during vacation periods.

31. "Le Pain quotidien," *Le Monde*, Numéro Spécial UNEF, 18 October 1963, p. 13.

32. In 1965 UNEF recommended that the stipend be something on the order of 450 N.F. per month (approximately $90) over a twelve-month period. *L'Allocation d'études, op. cit.*, p. 28.

33. Nicole Hautmont, *Habitat et vie étudiante* (Paris: Mutuelle Nationale des Etudiants de France, 1963), pp. 47–48. The breakdown of favorable responses within the various faculties was as follows: 73 per cent of the students in letters, 71 per cent of the students in science, 70 per cent of the students in medicine, and 59 per cent of the students in law.

34. Frank A. Pinner, "Student Trade-Unionism in France, Belgium, and Holland: Anticipatory Socialization and Role-Seeking," *Sociology of Education*, XXXVII, No. 3 (Spring 1964), 191.

35. Association Corporative des Etudiants en Droit (FNEF), *Projet de financement des études supérieures* (Paris, 1964). The irony of the FNEF's criticism of the *allocation d'études* as being Marxist is that the views of the FNEF and the Communist Party on the proposal are identical. Both propose a system based upon need.

36. Bertrand Girod de l'Ain, "L'Enseignement dans neuf pays 'developpés,'" *Le Monde Sélection Hebdomadaire*, 10–16 March 1966, p. 7.

37. Computed by the author from data in *L'Année politique, économique, sociale, et diplomatique en France 1965, op. cit.*, p. 398.

38. See W. R. Fraser, *Education and Society in Modern France* (London: Routledge and Kegan Paul, 1963), Chapter 4.

39. *Manifeste pour une réforme démocratique de l'enseignement supérieur, op. cit.*, pp. 16–17.

40. *Ibid.*, p. 16.

41. *Le Monde Sélection Hebdomadaire,* 9–15 March 1967, p. 10.
42. Jean Barale, "Les Etudiants d'Aix-en-Provence et la politique en Mai 1957," *Revue Française de Science Politique,* IX, No. 4 (December 1959), 967.
43. *Le Monde Sélection Hebdomadaire,* 9–15 March 1967, p. 10.
44. For interesting comments on the political consequences of the unemployment and neglect of intellectuals in India, see Edward Shils, "Influence and Withdrawal: The Intellectuals in Indian Political Development," in Dwaine Marvick, ed., *Political Decision-Makers* (New York: The Free Press of Glencoe, 1961), pp. 29–56.
45. See Ministère de l'Education Nationale, *La Réforme de l'enseignement* (Paris, 1966).
46. *Manifeste pour une réforme democratique de l'enseignement, op. cit.,* pp. 8–9.
47. De la Fournière and Borella, *op. cit.* Michel de la Fournière was the president of the minoritaire Bureau elected in July 1956. This was the first completely minoritaire Bureau elected since 1950. François Borella was elected president of UNEF by the General Assembly of October 1955 and held that office for several hours in an abortive attempt of the minoritaires to take control of the National Bureau. See Chapter 3, p. 30 of this work.
48. Gabriel A. Almond, "Introduction: A Functional Approach to Comparative Politics," in Gabriel A. Almond and James B. Coleman, eds., *The Politics of the Developing Areas* (Princeton: Princeton University Press, 1960), p. 37.
49. See Victor Brombert, *The Intellectual Hero: Studies in the French Novel, 1880–1955* (Philadelphia: J. B. Lippincott Company, 1960), Chapter 2 ("Toward a Portrait of the French Intellectual").
50. On the role of the "intellectuals" during the Dreyfus Affair see: Maurice Barrès, *Scènes et doctrines du nationalisme,* Vol. I (Paris: Librairie Plon, 1925); Maurice Barrès, "La Protestation des intellectuels!," *Le Journal* (1 February 1898), p. 1; Brombert, *op. cit.*; Cecile Delhorbe, *L'Affaire Dreyfus et les écrivains français* (Neuchatel: Editions Victor Attinger, 1923); Maurice Paleologue, *Journal de l'Affaire Dreyfus 1894–1899: l'Affaire Dreyfus et le Quai d'Orsay* (Paris: Plon, 1955); Charles Péguy, *De la Situation faite à l'histoire et à la sociologie dans les temps modernes* (1906) reprinted in *Oeuvres complètes de Charles Péguy,* Vol. III (Paris: Editions de la Nouvelle Revue Française, 1927); Charles Péguy, *Notre Jeunesse* (1910), reprinted, *op. cit.*; and the protests and the articles of Georges Clemenceau and Emile Zola in *L'Aurore* from 13 January 1898 to 17 January 1898.

    More general sources on the role of the intellectual in France are: Raymond Aron, *The Opium of the Intellectuals,* trans. Terence Kilmartin (New York: The Norton Library, 1962); Julian Benda, *The Betrayal of the Intellectuals,* trans. Richard Aldington (Boston: The

Beacon Press, 1955); Louis Bodin, *Les Intellectuels* (Paris: Presses Universitaires de France, 1962), p. 16; David Caute, *Communism and the French Intellectuals 1914–1960* (London: André Deutsch, 1964); Jean Kanapa, *Situation de l'intellectuel* (Paris: Editions Sociales, 1957); Herbert Luthy, "The French Intellectuals," *Encounter* (August 1955), pp. 5–15, reprinted in George B. Huszar, ed., *The Intellectuals: A Controversial Portrait* (Glencoe: The Free Press, 1960), pp. 444–458; Albert Thibaudet, *La République des professeurs* (Paris: Grasset, 1927). Also see: *Arguments*, No. 20 (summer 1960); *France-Forum*, Vol. XLI (June 1962); *Revue Française de Science Politique*, Vol. IX, No. 4 (December 1959).

51. At the Congress of 1966 a record number of sixty foreign student delegations were in attendance.

52. In 1963, 20.5 per cent of the national budget was devoted to the military and 14.1 per cent to education. Computed by the author from data in *Annuaire Statistique de la France 1966* (Paris: Institut National de la Statistique et des Etudes Economiques, 1967), p. 493.

53. In January 1967 an observer of the movement reported that the only political issue on which UNEF could make an effective appeal to French students was the war in Vietnam. *Le Monde*, 17 January 1967, p. 22.

54. Both the IUS and ISC meet in plenary sessions once every two years.

55. We have stated that it was doubtful that the minoritaires were aware of the relationship between the CIA and the ISC. In 1957 de la Fournière and Borella (*op. cit.*, pp. 160–161) called the ISC "the best international tribune." In 1961 Pierre Gaudez (*op. cit.*, pp. 182–183) wrote: "It appears today . . . as an organ in defense of the 'free world' against 'communist infiltration,' a second cousin of NATO and other family pacts. And yet, within the organization, great concessions are made in order not to chase the new unions of Africa, Asia and Latin America."

56. *Le Monde*, 9 July 1963, p. 5.

57. See Chapter 3, p. 58, above.

58. Gaudez, *op. cit.*, pp. 181–182. Gaudez, minoritaire president of UNEF in 1960–1961, adds in a footnote to the word "freedom" in the paragraph above: "If we refuse to 'die for freedom' it is because this word no longer has any meaning when regimes which use it practice genocide in Algeria or Angola or economic imperialism in Latin America. We are in agreement on this point with the national unions in the developing areas."

Chapter 5

Organization, Participation, and Control

We have maintained that postwar France would rank high on any scale which might be constructed to measure the scope and intensity of student activism. The most important channel of expression and interaction for the activists has been UNEF. However, this is not to say that all, or even most, students have responded to the conditions discussed in the last chapter by becoming militant members of UNEF. In this chapter we shall take a close look at UNEF's recruitment under both minoritaire and majoritaire leadership, as well as at the amount of participation within the organization.

Recruitment

Why the Size of an Organization Is Important

The size of an organization is important because it is a determinant of the legitimacy which will be accorded its claim to speak in the name of its category of people. What matters is not absolute size but the ratio between the actual and the potential membership of the organization. In democratic societies there tends to be a direct relationship between this ratio and a feeling of the moral obligation of the general society and its policy-makers to attend to the articulations of the organization. Thus a 1955 law stipulated that student associations be awarded representation on the Administrative Council of the CNO in proportion to their following among the student body.

The size of an organization also affects resources it will be able to bring to bear on the policy-making process. The major resources are votes, finances, and the manpower for direct action. Student organizations pose only a minor electoral threat, at least immediately, because many members are under the voting age. UNEF relies primarily on publicity campaigns which require both money and manpower.

The major source of UNEF's revenue has always been membership dues. For instance, if the entire subsidy of approximately $20,000 had been delivered in 1963–1964, it would have accounted for less than 25 per cent of the budget of the national organization. In that year the national organization received approximately 80 cents for each card sold to a regular UNEF member and approximately 20 cents for each card sold to a member of the Union des Grandes Ecoles; a total of approximately $64,000 in dues was forwarded by local AGE chapters to the national office. The local organizations kept the remainder of the membership fees, which generally ranged between $2 and $3 per member.

The cost of UNEF's ambitious programs far exceeds its revenue. By January 1967 the combined effect of the withheld subsidy and a serious decline in membership was the accumulation of debts totalling approximately $94,000 (470,000 N.F.).[1] It has been not an infrequent tactic for majoritaire AGES to play on this by withholding the national organization's portion of its membership dues, to protest the policies of minoritaire National Bureaux.

Good recruitment is also important to the leaders of a student- and environment-oriented organization because of the emphasis they place on the function of attitude formation among the students. In order to perform this function, the leaders must recruit the uncommitted and the antagonistic into the organization.

The Problem of Recruitment Faced by a Student- and Environment-Oriented Organization

The strategic difficulty which arises in recruiting is caused by the heterogeneity of viewpoints which the leaders must deal with. Unless the content of the message is very general, a bland appeal to take an interest in the affairs of the country (a kind of League of Women Voters appeal), a significant proportion of the student body will have political attitudes which lead them to reject the message, and the organization. The more specific and controversial the political positions taken, the greater will be the tendency of many of the uncommitted or differently committed to reject participation.

There is another problem that further complicates matters. For some students the legitimacy of a student organization is derived from the attention which it devotes to the corporate concerns of the students. For others, attention to corporate issues is not sufficient to legitimize the existence of the organization. When the latter group is large, as it has been in postwar France, the organization will lose support if it refuses to become controversially involved in environmental issues.

The breadth of support which a student- and environment-oriented organization can muster depends on several variables: the intensity and diversity of ideological commitment within the society; the nature of the specific noncorporate issues which arise; the balance of attention which the leadership gives to corporate and noncorporate issues; the success of the leadership in the corporate domain; the preservation of freedom of expression and competition within the organization; whether the opposition feels it is able to control some positions or force compromise; and the degree of affective attachment the organization's history and image can create.

People who disagree coexist in almost every organization. Sometimes, however, there arises what Robert A. Dahl calls symmetrical severe disagreement.[2] This is to say that at times a specific issue arises over which a substantial number of people disagree so intensely that coexistence is no longer possible. The cohesive ties to mutual corporate interests and the attachment to the history and image of the organization are undone, and it becomes impossible for the losers to accept electoral outcomes.

The Recruitment Performance of UNEF and FNEF

Table 5–1 presents approximations of the absolute membership figures of UNEF and of the percentage of the total student body which they represent. The organization experienced a healthy rate of growth during the first period of minoritaire control (1946–1950), during the period of absolute majoritaire control (1950–1953), and during the coalition period (1953–1956). The divisive noncorporate issues then were colonialism (especially over the war in Indochina) and UNEF's relationship with the International Union of Students.

Neither of these issues had the explosive effect which the Algerian crisis was to have. French prosecution of the war in Indochina was debated and at times condemned in 1948, but it never became the ultimate concern of UNEF. And by 1949 the minoritaires themselves, under pressure from the opposition, had reduced UNEF's role in the International Union of Students to that of observer and began to participate in the formation of the International Student Conference in 1950. The activists were polarized into two contending parties, but, up to 1956, the antagonists were able to coexist, compete, and accept the outcomes of elections in the one organization.

As we have seen, such was no longer the case once the Algerian issue was brought before UNEF. Because of the number of European French citizens residing in Algeria, its proximity to the mainland, its status as a *département* rather than a colony, and the earlier defeat of the French army in Indochina, intensity of feeling about the Algerian issue was greater than about Indochina. In addition, there were the constant counter-pressures exerted on the one hand by the well-organized Algerian student union and other sympathetic Arab student groups, and on the other by the European or non-Arab dominated student association at the University of Algiers. It is not surprising that this issue, which split the French political community and brought down the Fourth French Republic, also split UNEF. Whereas the organization claimed 88,000 members or 42 per cent of the student body in 1957, it claimed 3,000 fewer

TABLE 5-1   *Participation in* UNEF: *1945 to 1967*

CONGRESS	NUMBER OF STUDENTS IN INSTITUTIONS OF HIGHER EDUCATION [1]	APPROXIMATE MEMBERSHIP OF UNEF [2]	APPROXIMATE PERCENTAGE OF TOTAL STUDENT BODY AFFILIATED WITH UNEF
1945	123,000	25,000	20
1950	170,000 (est.)	42,000	25
1957	212,000	88,000	42
1963	328,000	85,000	26
1964	384,000	85,000	22
1967	460,000	49,000	11

1. Rounded to the nearest thousand. These figures include all students registered in the student insurance program. To obtain an approximate percentage of members among only those students who were enrolled in faculties and grandes écoles, 4 per cent should be added to the percentages in the last column.

2. Membership figures after 1957 include members of the Union des Grandes Ecoles which affiliated with UNEF in 1957–1958.

SOURCE: Membership and enrollment figures for 1945, 1950, and 1957 are taken from Jacques François Lefèvre, "L'Union Nationale des Etudiants de France depuis 1945" (unpublished thesis, Institut d'Etudes Politiques, Paris, 1958), pp. 26–27. Total enrollment figures for 1962–1963 and 1963–1964 are from UNEF—*Informations, Données Statistiques, 53ᵉ Congrès* (Paris, 1964). Membership figure for 1962–1963 is from UNEF's official membership files. The membership figure for 1963–1964 was calculated by the author on the basis of the report of the Financial Commission to the 1964 Congress on the revenue derived from the sale of membership cards.

In *Le Monde* (31 January 1967, p. 8) Frédéric Gaussen reported a 1966–1967 membership figure of 50,000. The 49,000 figure was calculated by the author from the membership figures used by UNEF in according votes to each AGE in July 1967. These data were graciously provided by M. Pierre Montacié, treasurer of UNEF. It should be pointed out, however, that M. Montacié feels that the figures do not accurately represent the size of the organization. He estimates the membership to be closer to 70,000 than to 49,000 (or approximately 15 per cent of the student body) but admits that this is a highly impressionistic estimate. On an equally impressionistic basis, this writer feels that while the 49,000 figure could be too low the 70,000 estimate is too high. Since there is really no way of obtaining a figure with an absolute certainty of accuracy the official figure is used in this table.

members, less than 26 per cent of the student body, in 1963. In terms of the percentage of the potential membership actually recruited, UNEF was not much larger than it had been in 1950. Furthermore, its monopoly on student trade-unionism had been lost.

The minoritaire leadership was well aware of the risk it was taking by bringing the issue of Algeria before the whole of UNEF. This was why not until four years after the minoritaires assumed power in the organization was a firm position taken. Between 1956 and 1960, however, the intensity of commitment of the minoritaires had grown because of the prolongation of the war, the reports of widespread use of torture, the mistreatment of Algerian nationalist students in France, and the constantly increasing draft quotas and troops commitments. Moreover, some minoritaire activists, frustrated by the unwillingness of the organization to commit itself, were finding alternative channels of engagement: some had even joined FLN support networks. The situation had reached the point where the minoritaires had to decide whether to continue appeasing the majoritaires in order to avoid a threatened defection or to follow their own ideological inclinations and avoid disaffection within their own ranks.

Moreover, the minoritaire leadership was not convinced that the real issue for many majoritaires was corporatism versus political engagement. There was a grave suspicion that many of the majoritaires were political conservatives who favored the prosecution of the war. Since these people could not have won in a prowar-antiwar confrontation, the minoritaires feared that the opposition was pursuing a strategy of indirectly neutralizing the majority on the issue. Pierre Gaudez, president of UNEF in 1960–1961, accused the majoritaire AGE of Paris-Law of practicing "tactical apoliticism." [3] He contended that the AGE was guided by a "naive, primary, and aggressive anticommunism. . . . When they do not succeed they pick up their marbles and slam the door behind them." [4] There was some basis for this suspicion: majoritaire delegates to the Conseil d'Administration had voted to ratify the protests which the minoritaire National Bureau had made against Soviet military intervention in Hungary in 1956.[5]

The most drastic decline in support for UNEF, however, did not occur until after the confrontations with the government in 1963–1964. Because UNEF was thereafter deprived both of access to governmental decision-makers and of its subsidy, it was not able to function effectively even as a corporate interest group. And there is no longer any specific noncorporate issue around which students can be rallied. As has been suggested, the result of this frustrating position has been a fragmentation of the minoritaires over the question of how to emerge from their present powerlessness. A group which has been immobilized to this extent is bound to encounter difficulties in recruiting.

On the other hand, the Fédération Nationale des Etudiants de France has not proved to be an effective rival of UNEF. During its first year of existence, 1961–1962, it claimed to have 30,000 members; by 1963–1964 it was claiming a membership of 40,000. As has been indicated [6] the first claim was made even before the FNEF had a chance to begin selling membership cards or to present its candidates. The second claim has been disputed by UNEF's leaders. In 1963–1964 they maintained that the FNEF probably had 15,000 members. In fact, by awarding four student seats on the Administrative Council of the CNO to UNEF and only one to the FNEF in his decree of October 1963, the Minister of Education tacitly admitted that FNEF's membership was no larger than 25 per cent of UNEF's. Government sources indicate that, while the FNEF was still claiming 40,000 members in 1965, it had actually sold only 13,985 membership cards.[7] Since 1961–1962 the FNEF has probably maintained a membership rate between one-fourth and one-fifth of that maintained by UNEF. There are several reasons for its limited appeal.

First, the FNEF has constantly felt the need to defend itself against the charge that it is not an independent student organization but a creation of the Gaullist government. By blatantly extending it preferential treatment, the Gaullists have probably done the FNEF more harm than good. It should be pointed out, however, that the FNEF has often been critical of the government's education policies since the Algerian War and that it suffered just as much as UNEF from the ministerial decree of October 1963. After its exaggerated membership claims, to receive the same representation on the Administrative Council of the CNO as the Union des

Grandes Ecoles and the Fédération Nationale des Associations d'Elèves en Grandes Ecoles was a source of considerable embarrassment to the FNEF.

Second, the FNEF has not provided a comfortable haven for those students whose true wish was to avoid ideological issues entirely. Many of the FNEF's leaders and activists have been political conservatives or rightists. They have given the organization's campaign against UNEF a heavily anti-Marxist and anticommunist orientation—even to the point of branding the popular proposal for an *allocation d'études* as being Marxist.[8]

Third, the membership of the FNEF is heavily concentrated in professional schools. Its corporate interests therefore tend to be directed toward future professional life. Students in letters and science, who outnumber students in professional schools by almost two to one, tend to have a more immediate conception of corporate interests. Largely as a result of this, there tends to be a greater feeling of identity or similarity of corporate interest across disciplines in letters and science than across professional schools. Thus the FNEF is a much less cohesive organization than UNEF. Many of the corporate concerns of its members are handled more effectively by autonomous associations of students in the different professional faculties. For all these reasons the largest AGE in UNEF, that of Paris-Science, has remained an isolated, embattled, and somewhat alienated majoritaire AGE within UNEF, despite the continuing attempts of the leaders of the FNEF to entice it into their organization.[9]

Outside of UNEF and the FNEF there are a few corporatist student associations at individual institutions which have refused to affiliate with either national organization. In a survey conducted in 1961–1962 and 1962–1963, 13 per cent of the male sample and 3 per cent of the female sample belonged to such independent organizations. In the same survey 52 per cent of the male sample and 41 per cent of the female sample belonged to UNEF, to the FNEF, or to an independent corporatist union.[10]

Participation, Bureaucracy, and Democracy within UNEF

Why One Would Expect a Small Minority to Participate Actively

There are several reasons one would expect only a small minority of UNEF's members to participate actively in the decision-making and administrative processes of the organization. First, this has been the norm in most organizations which have been the subject of empirical investigation since the appearance in 1915 of Roberto Michels' study of the German Social Democratic Party.[11]

Second, the successful leader must be persuasive, be an efficient administrator, and possess a high degree of tolerance for competition and conflict.[12] Some people possess talents and personality traits which make them attractive and effective leaders, some do not; some people thrive on competition and conflict, most people prefer to avoid them.

Third, leadership and activism are time-consuming and often costly—and there are generally other pressures upon the individual.[13] This is particularly true of students. The French student must study hard in order to avoid joining the 66 per cent who fail to take a degree. He must, beyond that, maintain a high level of academic performance in order to keep his scholarship (if he has one) and his rights to health insurance and student benefits. And, as we have seen, many French students are also employed. Michel Mousel, UNEF's president in 1963–1964, lost two years of study and his scholarship as a result of his service to the organization at the local and national levels,[14] for he who hopes to attain national office must begin his activism rather early in his academic career.

Fourth, leadership in UNEF does not hold the prospect of long-term rewards. An activist in a labor or professional organization can make a career, and often a financially rewarding one, out of organizational activity. This is impossible in a student organization because of the short duration of the individual's student life. UNEF's leaders are not salaried and, as we shall see, their tenure is short.

Furthermore, leadership and activism in UNEF are not viewed as steppingstones to careers in government or political life the way leadership in the United States National Student Association has been. Largely because of the students' own lack of enthusiasm for the traditional political parties, leadership in UNEF has more often than not led to a dead end. As Jacques Frèyssinet wrote in the summer of 1960, approximately three months after he left the national presidency of UNEF:

> There is a problem which bothers us a great deal. The student movement has been sending its retired leaders into the world for over ten years now. It is disturbing to note that most of them have not found places in which to continue their activity.
>
> Political parties, unions, and diverse organizations have claimed only a few. The others become disillusioned and abandon [their activism].[15]

Fifth, the very concept of formal organization imposes limits on participation. UNEF performs three functions: it is an interest group, a service organization, and, under the minoritaires, an institution for formation and articulation of political attitudes. In an organization as large as UNEF, none of these functions could be performed under conditions of complete political equality. A certain amount of hierarchy and delegation of authority is necessary. The danger is that the organizational apparatus can become so complicated and the proceedings so esoteric that non-leaders find it difficult to keep abreast of organizational issues and to hold leaders accountable. Minoritaire leaders have constantly criticized themselves for allowing what they refer to as the "bureaucratization" of UNEF to develop. It is therefore appropriate to turn to a more detailed consideration of that "bureaucracy," the formal organization of UNEF.

Every member of UNEF, honorary members aside, is so by virtue of having purchased membership in an Association Générale des Etudiants (AGE). In 1963–1964 there were 37 AGES and 16 Associations des Elèves de l'Ecole, the Union des Grandes Ecoles' equivalents of the AGE. Each of the provincial universities has a single AGE which groups together students from all faculties and grandes écoles within the academic district. In Paris each of the faculties and some of the grandes écoles have their own associations.

The AGE may be federated or unitary. A unitary AGE is one in which a single bureau is elected by all membership cardholders. With the exception of the AGE at the Faculty of Letters, the chapters at Parisian faculties and at the Institut d'Etudes Politiques are unitary structures. The AGE at the Faculty of Letters in Paris and at most provincial universities are federations of students in different disciplines and curricula.

The AGE at Poitiers adopted a federal form of organization in 1964–1965. Although there do exist slight variations among forms of federation in provincial AGE's, a description of Poitiers' organization will give the reader a general idea of the nature and lines of federation in the provincial AGE.

The AGE is a federation of five associations of students, each belonging to a single faculty or general type of program. They are: the Union des Etudiants en Lettres de Poitiers, the Corporation des Etudiants en Sciences, the Union des Etudiants en Droit et Sciences Economiques, the Association des Etudiants Techniciens de Poitiers, and the Association des Etudiants Préparationnaires. The Union des Etudiants en Lettres is further divided into associations of students in several areas of study. These divisions are the same as those which exist at the Faculty of Letters in Paris. There are associations of students in history and geography, modern languages, social sciences, linguistics and classical languages, and *propédeutique* (one year prefaculty preparation). The members of each lower association elect a bureau, which in turn elects one of its members as a representative to the Administrative Council of the Union des Etudiants en Lettres.

Except for the students in letters, the basic unit is the general assembly. The general assembly is composed of all cardholders in the faculty or general program who wish to attend. The general assemblies meet twice each academic year. The first meetings are held in November, at the beginning of the school year. At this time the general assemblies elect administrative councils. The second meetings are held before the national meetings of the *offices* to which the associations belong. At these meetings the students determine what issues regarding curricula and preprofessional training they want discussed at the national level of the *office*.

The several administrative councils elect the general assembly of the entire AGE, a body of between thirty and forty members

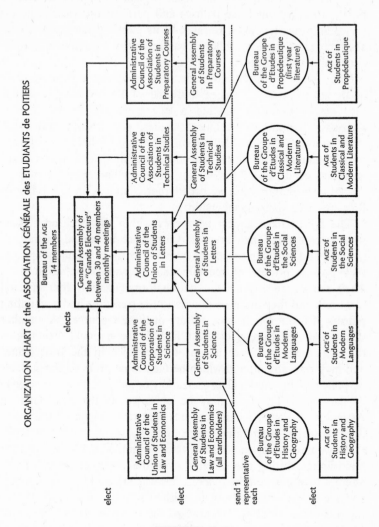

ORGANIZATION CHART of the ASSOCIATION GÉNÉRALE des ETUDIANTS de POITIERS

FIGURE 5-1

which meets once per month. Their functions are to determine the orientation and policy of the local organization, and to elect a bureau to carry out these policies and perform the various necessary administrative tasks. Because of its electoral task, the general assembly is referred to, rather elegantly, as the Assemblée Générale des Grandes Electeurs.

The *offices* of UNEF are structures which group all students according to general areas of study. As of 1963–1964 there were nine *offices* grouping students in letters, science, medicine, law, pharmacy, commerce, technical studies, paramedical and social work studies, and *propédeutique*. Each *office* holds a national meeting annually at which problems peculiar to its area of study are considered. The Parisian AGE chapters and sections of provincial AGE chapters are accorded representation in the *office* in proportion to their membership.

The *offices* have almost no power within the decision-making process of UNEF. Their area of competence is limited to the immediate and peculiar corporate interests of their membership, and they possess powers of recommendation and consultation only. They are dependent on the national organization for financial resources and they are accountable to the treasurer and accounting officers of UNEF for the expenditure of these resources. A member of the National Bureau of UNEF attends the national meetings of the *offices*. He possesses a consultative voice in the proceedings and may veto any motion which he feels is contrary to the statutes or policy of the national organization or outside the competence of the *office*. The veto may be appealed at the next General Assembly of UNEF, where the president or delegate of the *office* does possess a consultative voice.

As we have seen, one of the strategies employed by the dissident *majoritaires* during the debates over the Algerian issue was to attempt to strengthen the *offices*. This was rejected by the majority, and the professional *offices* diminished in size considerably when the dissidents withdrew and formed the FNEF in 1961. The *office* of dentistry students disappeared entirely. Within the FNEF the *offices* have considerably more power than they do in UNEF. In 1964 after their control over UNEF had been firmly entrenched, the *minoritaires* themselves were giving serious consideration to strengthening UNEF's *offices*.

On the national plane the two important bodies are the General Assembly and the National Bureau. Before it was abolished in November 1959, an Administrative Council served as a check on the performance of the National Bureau.

The General Assembly, like the local assemblies, determines the policy of the organization, and elects and serves as a check on the behavior of the National Bureau. It meets four times a year. Three regular General Assembly meetings are held in Paris, in November, February, and July, and generally last only a weekend. Another General Assembly meeting is held during the Easter vacation, in a different city each year, and lasts about a week: it is designated the Congress of UNEF. Special Assemblies may be convoked at any time by the National Bureau and must be convoked if one-fourth of the AGES petition.

There are various consultative members of the Assembly, who may participate in the debates but may not cast a vote. They are: members of the National Bureau; officers of the *offices*; the accountants (*commissaires aux comptes*) of UNEF; the judicial counsellor of UNEF (a graduate law student who extends statutory and procedural advice); the presidents and members of the bureaux of the Mutuelle Nationale des Etudiants de France (student insurance administration), of the Union des Grandes Ecoles, and of the Fédération des Etudiants de Paris (an association of presidents of student organizations in Paris); honorary members (generally former officers who wish to continue to take an interest in UNEF); and invited guests of the Assembly. Paid administrators, unpaid workers in the national office, and delegates from foreign student associations may participate in discussions which directly concern them. An AGE may send additional consultative representatives, so long as they do not exceed in number the votes possessed by the AGE or the number of committees of the Assembly, whichever is greater.

The deliberative or voting members of the Assembly are the officers of the local AGE chapters. Each delegation is led by the president, who casts a block vote. Under the statutes of 1950 the larger chapters were severely underrepresented. By 1959 over one-half of the AGES had over 2,000 members, but about two-thirds of the votes were controlled by chapters with fewer than 2,000 members.[16] In 1959 votes were reapportioned. A completely proportional distribution of votes would have given an absolute majority to six mammoth AGES: Lyon, Lille, Toulouse, Paris-Letters, Paris-Medicine, and Paris-Science. In order to avoid this, a "lightly corrected" representation plan proposed by Paris-Law was accepted. This plan gave an AGE with from 500 to 5,000 members one vote for every 100 members; an AGE having more than 5,000 members received the same number of votes for the first 5,000 plus one supplementary vote for every 200 additional members. In 1962 about two-thirds of the votes were in the hands of chapters with more than 2,000 members.[17]

The obvious defect in the scheme was that AGES which did not have at least 500 members, of which there were seven in 1963–1964, were completely unrepresented. This would of course discourage the formation of new AGE chapters and the growth of small ones. It was thus decided at the Congress of 1960 that every AGE outside of the greater Parisian area would receive one vote if they had 201 members. After the correction was made, only one AGE at the 1960 Congress, the Fédération des Ecoles de Commerce, was without a vote; this Parisian AGE had 428 members.[18] In 1963–1964 one Parisian chapter, the Cartel des Ecoles Para-Medicales et Sociales, and one or two provincial ones found themselves unrepresented.

The National Bureau makes administrative preparations for the assemblies. It presents an agenda which the Assembly may accept or reject. The normal order of business is as follows. The president of UNEF opens the meeting. The credentials of each AGE delegation are validated or rejected. The order of the day is adopted. Committees are then established to consider various types of subject matter and report on them to the entire Assembly. All of these items of business are conducted in closed session.

In a Congress this would be followed by a plenary session in which outgoing national officers would deliver reports which the Congress would vote to accept or reject. The regular Assembly, however, adjourns immediately so that the committees and the *offices* can meet. Then an open plenary session is held at which the committee reports are debated and policy is voted. If national officers resign or if a vote of censure against an officer is introduced, the Assembly goes into closed session to debate the issue and, if needs be, to elect a new officer.

Each Assembly determines the number and subject matter of its own committees. The General Assembly of February 1964 established eight committees to deal with various subjects, which include: culture, sports, recruitment and communication, university affairs, internal affairs, the *allocation d'études*, international affairs, and administrative and discipline problems. Committees may meet jointly to consider issues which overlap. In February 1964 the sports and international affairs committees met separately and then held a joint meeting on the problem of whether or not to participate in international games from which teams from Israel and Taiwan had been barred.[19]

Both deliberative and consultative members may participate in the work of the committees, including the election of their own president. Motions are presented for the committees' consideration. Regardless of its size, each AGE in attendance possesses one vote in committee, and a simple majority suffices to carry a motion to the floor, where the matter is presented to the open session of the Assembly for debate and vote. If, however, a committee unanimously adopts a motion, it is considered adopted by the Assembly without debate. Such a motion may be debated, rejected, or amended by the Assembly only if five AGE chapters present a written demand to the presiding officer of the session. If the issues fall within their competence, five *offices* may present such a demand.

Election of officers and votes of confidence or censure are conducted by secret ballot. Otherwise a show of hands or a voice vote is sufficient. A change in the statutes or charter requires a two-thirds majority. On all other issues a simple majority is sufficient.

The full sessions are often quite tense and acrimonious. Delegates are constantly running here and there to confer with other delegates from other AGES. Speakers address the entire body as "camarades" and use the familiar second person ("tu" and "toi") in debate. However, the use of familiar terminology, something which has spread to the student culture generally, does not soften a bitter expression of disagreement over policy.

The tone of the Congress is somewhat different from that of the regular General Assembly. The stakes are always higher, because every Congress elects an entirely new National Bureau. It is also a more festive occasion, because the students feel they own the small towns as no one ever owns Paris, and numerous foreign student delegations and press representatives are in attendance. And since the Congress runs for a week, the representatives do not feel the pressure of time as much as they do at the weekend General Assemblies.

The executive body of UNEF is the National Bureau. Among its functions are: the execution of policy decided upon by the General Assembly; the preparation of the budget of the national organization; the representation, when it is invited, of UNEF at the centers of governmental decision-making; the representation of UNEF on the Administrative Council of the CNO and on other official and advisory bodies; the preparation of the agenda and physical facilities for the General Assemblies; and the publicizing of UNEF's demands.

The 1959 statutes provide for a National Bureau of fifteen members assisted by two accounting officers and a judicial advisor. The statutes establish and define the posts of president, secretary general, and treasurer. The General Assembly decides upon the division of labor among the vice-presidents and deputy vice-presidents. However, members of the Union des Grandes Ecoles must occupy the vice-presidency or the deputy vice-presidency of both internal and university affairs, posts which are always established. All officers must be of French nationality and must enjoy full civil rights. The president and the treasurer must be at least twenty-one years of age. The judicial advisor must possess a *licence* in law.

Nonincumbents must have the nominations of their AGES. In fact almost all are presidents of their chapters; the key to success is thus informal backing from the more powerful AGES, which is obtained through the party system. The election is by secret ballot in closed session. Each office is filled separately, with the presidency being filled first. On the first ballot a two-thirds majority is required for election; on the second an absolute majority is needed and on the third a plurality suffices. If only one candidate is nominated for a post, an "aye" and "nay" vote may be taken.

All officers are elected for a one-year term from the date of the Congress. They are, however, subject to censure and to recall by any of the three intervening General Assemblies or by a special General Assembly. Upon completion of his term of office, an officer is expected to deliver a report on his activities to the Congress. The Congress then votes to approve or disapprove the report. If the report is approved the officer may officially be re-elected without the nomination of his AGE.

The president presides at the meetings of the Bureau and represents UNEF in any legal action in which it might become involved. The Bureau regularly meets every fifteen days. However, the president may convene a meeting of the Bureau at any time and must convene one if one-third of the members request it in writing. The presidents of the Mutuelle Nationale des Etudiants de France and the Union des Grandes Ecoles have the right to attend Bureau meetings or to send representatives when the agenda touches upon their domains.

While the Bureau is the major executive body of the national organization, it is also explicitly vested with the responsibility for policy-making between meetings of the General Assembly. The next General Assembly must then decide, when it meets, either to ratify or to reject the decisions made in the interval by the Bureau.

Factors Counteracting the Tendency Toward Oligarchical Control in UNEF

There are two factors which counteract the tendency toward oligarchical control in UNEF: the nature of the role of student, and a strong commitment to democratic norms.

Two attributes of the student role militate against the development of the type of relatively permanent oligarchy which Michels describes. First, the duration of one's life as student is brief: the student is preparing for a career, not engaging in one. French rules and legislation discourage individuals from deliberately prolonging their studies by imposing penalties for nonadvancement and by depriving people over twenty-six years of age of certain student benefits. Second, the academic demands made upon the student are pressing. Local leaders continue their studies while they serve and are generally very busy people. Members of the National Bureau generally take off precious time from their studies to serve. They may serve before or after they have received the *licence*, but they must be enrolled as students when elected. After their service on the National Bureau they generally either resume their studies to finish the *licence*, take an advanced degree, or enter military service.[20] Thus, UNEF's leaders do not "live in the [organization] . . ., grow old and die in its service." [21]

At the national level, when Jean-François Nallet, the outgoing president, agreed to head a "care-taker" bureau at the Congress of 1966, it was the first time that a president of UNEF had served more than one term since the minoritaires gained access to the National Bureau in July 1953. Before this, one minoritaire president had served for three years (April 1946–April 1949) and one majoritaire president had served for two years (November 1950–November 1952).[22]

At the local level, questionnaire responses from five provincial and two Parisian AGES indicate that the average length of service of a member of their bureaux, including all positions held, is between two and three years. Five of the presidents were completing their first year of service as president, and two were completing their second year. All declared that one year was the average length of service of a president of their chapter (one did not respond). When asked to state the longest period of service of an individual president that they could remember, their answers ranged from one to two years. Jacques François Lefèvre reports the case of a president of a Parisian AGE who served until he was thirty-two years old; this he cites as an extreme deviation from the norm.[23]

However, the rapid rate of turnover of UNEF's leadership has two disadvantages. First, leaders have little time to learn routines and leadership skills in office. Thus they are at a disadvantage when dealing with more seasoned organization leaders in other private associations or in government. Second, the rapid rate of turnover leaves outsiders, with whom UNEF leaders want to deal, uncertain about the stability of agreements and relationships. A prominent labor leader expressed concern over this problem in an interview with the author. In the words of this professional unionist, "when one deals with UNEF one never knows with whom one will be dealing from one year to the next." [24]

The second factor which counteracts the tendency toward oligarchy is the very strong commitment of the organization to democratic norms. According to Truman, Dahl, and Lindblom, the shared commitment of the members and leaders to democratic norms is the major impediment to a complete surrender to oligarchy

in most organizations.[25] This anti-oligarchical attitude is the product
of the socialization processes of the general culture. More precisely,
it means that the leaders and members share the view that the
former should be held accountable to the latter. The attitude
manifests itself within an organization in a high degree of freedom
of expression and competition, a system of regular and fairly
frequent elections in which every member possesses the same
voting power, and the acceptance of electoral outcomes by both
members and leaders.

The *minoritaire* commitment to democratic norms has an unusual
dimension, like that of the advocates of "participatory democracy"
in New Left groups in the United States. For the *minoritaires* it
does not suffice that all members can, if they wish, participate
actively in the life of the organization. In their fundamentalist view
of democracy and their commitment to political equality, a low
rate of active participation within the organization seriously reduces its moral legitimacy. As Michel Mousel stated in his presidential report to the Congress of 1964, UNEF's ". . . true vocation [is] that of *un syndicalisme de masse.*" The leadership must
therefore interpret a low rate of participation as a personal failure
at performing a major function, attitude formation.

The commitment to democratic norms is reflected both by the
statutes of the organization and by the behavior of its leadership.
Let us examine some of the many specific statutory and behavioral
manifestations of this commitment, a commitment which is one
major defining characteristic of UNEF.

First, membership in UNEF is open, and members cannot be
excluded from the organization because they differ with the policy
positions of the leadership. The statutes of the national organization provide that no student, "except for grave reasons or other
syndical affiliation," may be refused the right to membership in
his institution's AGE. In fact the only students who are not permitted to purchase UNEF membership cards are those who are
known to be members of the rival Fédération Nationale des Etudiants de France and the Fédération Nationale des Associations
d'Eleves en Grandes Ecoles. As we have seen, all other students
are most strongly urged to join the organization and to become
activists in it.

Second, the flow of information from the leadership to the actual and potential members is copious. The national organization regularly publishes a formal magazine, *21·27: l'Etudiant de France*, which carries articles about UNEF, educational problems, and national and international issues. It also publishes a series of documents, *Unef-Informations*: these include the transcripts of the proceedings of UNEF's congresses, statistical information pertaining to student life and the educational system, and explanations of the national organization's positions on important issues. In addition to these two publications the National Bureau publishes each year a UNEF edition of *Le Monde*, which contains signed articles by the officers and, sometimes, by officers of the student insurance administration. Aside from these intra-organizational communications, the student can learn much about the national organization from the careful press coverage which it receives.

At the local level most AGEs distribute newsletters to bring their membership and the general student body up to date on the activities of both the local and national organizations. They also hold assemblies, open to all members, which permit a two way flow of information between leaders and non-leaders. The referendum is another means that some local leaders employ to obtain "feedback" from the members on particular issues. Frequently it is used when the leadership is considering calling a strike. The decentralized federation which constitutes some AGE chapters is a structure designed to bring the most people into the active life of the organization.

Nevertheless, the primary means of assuring accountability of leaders to non-leaders in any organization is the electoral process. Leaders must be convinced that they will be removed from office or not be reelected if their behavior deviates from what the majority of the members find desirable or acceptable. And numerous aspiring leaders must be available to offer alternative policy choices.

The statutes of the national organization require every AGE to adopt a democratic procedure for electing leaders. It is urged that local AGES adopt a federal form of organization and hold elections annually for every office (the annual renewal of one-third of the bureau mandates at Paris-Law is frowned upon). Also precise conditions are specified which must be met before the electoral procedure can be considered democratic.

So that all members who so desire may present candidacies, the time for such presentation and the time and place of balloting must be posted in public at least ten days in advance of the election. The right to vote is limited to members, but every member who presents his UNEF and student identification cards and signs the voting list must be given a printed ballot to mark in secret. The counting of ballots must take place under the supervision of representatives of all candidates. The candidate with the greatest number of votes must be declared the winner.

If a candidate should feel that unfair procedures have been employed in an election he may request an investigation by the Control Commission of UNEF. This body, which may also enter a case on its own initiative, is headed by the Judicial Counsellor of UNEF and composed of four delegates and their alternates, all appointed by the General Assembly of UNEF. The commission may choose to oversee elections only if the contending candidates are not opposed, but it always has the right to conduct an on-the-premises investigation after an election. If both parties to the dispute accept intervention by the commission, it may render a verdict directly. If not, it reports its findings to the General Assembly.

The General Assembly can invoke sanctions if chapter leaders refuse to follow the nationally prescribed electoral procedures or refuse to abide by the statutes of their own AGE. Four penalties may be imposed: (1) an injunction directed at the AGE, (2) a warning directed at the chapter as a whole or at the responsible individuals, (3) a censure motion, again directed against the chapter or the responsible individuals, perhaps supplemented by depriving them of the right to vote at General Assembly meetings, and (4) temporary or permanent expulsion of responsible individuals from UNEF.

An actual case of action taken against an individual AGE for violation of its own statutes and for undemocratic behavior arose early in 1964. About 2,300 students petitioned the majoritaire bureau of Paris-Science to call a special general assembly.[26] The petitioners were minoritaires who claimed that the opposition of the bureau to the policies of the national organization did not represent the sentiment of the students at the faculty. The bureau of the AGE refused to convoke the desired assembly, maintaining that the request was irregular and did not have the support of the 25 per cent of the members which, according to statute, would have made it obligatory to call together an assembly.

At issue was the base from which to calculate the proportionate strength of the petitioners. The Control Commission was asked to investigate and to report to the Congress in April. At the General Assembly in February the AGE had reported a 1962–1963 membership figure of 8,000. For the Congress, however, it reported a membership of 12,000. The bureau of Paris-Science insisted that the new membership figure should be used and that, since 2,300 is not 25 per cent of 12,000, it was under no obligation to convoke an assembly. The Control Commission determined that 8,000 was the proper figure and recommended that Paris-Science be temporarily deprived of its voting rights at the Congress. The Congress accepted the finding of the commission but decided to reduce the penalty to a censure for undemocratic behavior.[27]

The issue was a delicate one politically. Paris-Science is the largest AGE in UNEF and has been consistently majoritaire. Though it has never threatened to leave UNEF, it has often proved a thorn in the side of the minoritaire leadership and a frustration to its minoritaire members. The latest move of the AGE's bureau, and the one which undoubtedly had provoked the petition, had been its withdrawal from the demonstration during the visit of President Segni and its public denunciation of the organization for its behavior during the visit.

A significant sidelight to this conflict was that the government-controlled radio and television network, the Radio-Television Française (RTF), had anticipated the expulsion of the Paris-Science AGE. In a blatant attempt to portray the minoritaires as intolerant and undemocratic, the network decided to focus on this one issue at the Congress. The president of UNEF, Michel Mousel, and the president of the AGE at the Faculty of Science were cornered by reporters and cameramen as they left the session at which the AGE was censured. A television reporter, reading from a previously prepared list of questions, asked Mousel why Paris-Science had been expelled from UNEF. The president of UNEF walked away from the cameras without uttering a word. He later explained to the Congress that he did so because it was obvious that the RTF was concerned only to embarrass UNEF.[28]

The microphone was then turned over to the president of the AGE, who explained the position of his bureau. This was the only coverage of UNEF's 1964 Congress to which television viewers were treated on the popular Sunday Television Journal on 5 April 1964. UNEF issued a press release protesting the tactics of the government in using the RTF as a political weapon. The incident was publicized in *Le Monde*, and later the RTF did broadcast UNEF's press release and offered Mousel time to expound the position of his organization.[29]

We have already seen that the mandates of national officers expire after one year and that the officers are subject to recall at any of the three intervening General Assemblies. Indeed, should a sufficient number of AGE chapters feel that an officer is deserving of immediate dismissal, there is provision for calling a special General Assembly and passing a motion of censure.

What is most important, however, is the fact that the competition for office is real. Minoritaires and majoritaires regularly contest one another in local AGE elections. The majoritaire "party" has recently been revitalized by victories at the Faculty of Medicine (1963–1964) and the Institut d'Etudes Politiques (1964–1965) in Paris.

Moreover, changeovers of control of the national apparatus have been frequent, compared with most organizations. Lipset, Trow, and Coleman contend that a rare specimen of a democratic union is the International Typographical Union; it is democratic because it has utilized about three hundred referenda since 1900 and has a two-party system in which a changeover in control has occurred seven times between 1898 and 1954.[30] In UNEF's two-party system, by comparison, there have been three instances of complete changeover of control of the National Bureau and one instance of a coalition since only 1945. Interestingly enough, three of these four changes in control occurred before the one-year terms of the present incumbents had expired. When national officers lose majority support in UNEF, they fall immediately from power.

Actual Levels of Participation within UNEF

Thus far we have discussed the recruitment performance of UNEF, the factors conducive to oligarchy in the organization, and the factors which counteract the tendencies toward oligarchy. We have seen that UNEF is a highly democratic organization, in that all of its members are able to participate and are encouraged to do so. There is a healthy degree of competition within the organization and electoral outcomes are the major determinants of policy. Twice in the recent history of the organization, those who felt that they could not tolerate electoral outcomes have left the organization en masse. The majority policy did, however, prevail, and the organization survived the defections.

The final question on these matters is, what is meant by the word "majority" as it is used in the last sentence? Obviously it refers to the "majority" of only those members who participate in the affairs of the organization at least to the point of expressing preferences. Several items on the questionnaire which the author distributed to AGE presidents in 1965–1966 were designed to determine levels of actual as opposed to nominal participation. Utilizable responses to such items—concerned with voting and assembly and meeting attendance—were returned by the presidents of two Parisian AGES, two Parisian chapters of the Union des Grandes Ecoles, and five provincial AGES. The responses indicate that voting is for many the predominant form of active participation. But the variation is great, from less than 10 to about 80 per cent of the members. Attendance at assemblies and meetings in these chapters is practiced by between 7 and 30 per cent of the members. Of the five presidents who supplied estimated figures on assembly and meeting attendance, four reported a decline from previous years and one reported that the number attending had remained about the same.

In an attempt to arrive at some idea of the percentage of the entire student body and of the membership which might be considered militant, the following question was included in the questionnaire: "Militants: approximately how many students have shown a desire to belong to the bureau or to work seriously for the AGE this year?" Responses by the presidents of two Parisian and four provincial AGES indicated that, at these six institutions, about 1.5 per cent of the aggregated student bodies and about 5 per cent of the aggregated union membership were considered militants.

Participation in UNEF thus takes a pyramidal form. At the top of the pyramid are the approximately 5 per cent of the members who are considered militants. These are generally the leaders and those who aspire to leadership positions. This group formulates the policy alternatives to be presented to the membership. Below them is a layer which probably includes between 25 and 35 per cent of the membership. These are attentive members who feel a fairly strong sense of identification with the movement, regularly participate in elections and/or meetings, but do not seek leadership positions. The base of the pyramid probably includes between 60 and 70 per cent of the membership. These members do not closely identify with the organization; if they do participate in elections or other organizational activities, their participation is irregular. They are, relatively or completely, passive members.

Why would the bottom group bother to request membership and pay membership dues? Nicole Hautmont attempts to explain the low sense of identification, which she claims to find among a significant segment of student union members, exclusively on the basis of a consumer motive.[31] Various services are offered to the members by the different AGES. Among them may be: *polycopiés* (at a rather substantial cost), assistance in finding housing, tickets for movies and other forms of entertainment at discount prices, travel discounts and organized trips, and the right to purchase goods at the cooperative which the national organization maintains in Paris.

While some nonparticipating members undoubtedly come into the organization solely or largely to obtain these services, this does not seem a sufficient or even a primary explanation of nonparticipation or irregular participation. First, most services provided by AGES are made available to all students by the Comité National des Oeuvres. That the services rendered by AGES are not indispensable is indicated by the fact that a majority of students choose to live without them. The most important service, where the AGE chooses and is able to provide it, is undoubtedly the *polycopié*. Second, sole reliance on the consumer explanation simply ignores the fact that it is common for people to support financially interest associations in order to accord them resources and legitimacy without becoming involved in the internal lives of the organizations or feeling any great degree of identification with them.[32] These members have a favorable image of the organization, sympathize with its general goals (at least some of them), and trust that its work will continue to be favorable without their personal participation in the decision process.

In summary then, UNEF is an organization in which there is a high degree of freedom of expression and competition, in which there exists a system of regular and frequent elections, in which every member possesses the right to one vote, and in which the leaders and policies which receive the majority of votes prevail. The policy process is thus an open one. But, for reasons which we have discussed, not all members choose to exercise their right to participate actively. For some members, including the minoritaire leadership, this reduces the moral value of the organization and its decisions. But the very fact that the leadership is concerned and engages in self-criticism is indicative of the strength of UNEF's commitment to democratic norms. It would probably be difficult to find many large organizations in which democratic norms are as honored in theory and in practice.

NOTES

1. *Le Monde*, 31 January 1967, p. 8.
2. Robert A. Dahl, *A Preface to Democratic Theory* (Chicago: The University of Chicago Press, 1956), p. 98.
3. Pierre Gaudez, *Les Etudiants* (Paris: Julliard, 1961), pp. 52–54. On the other hand, Gaudez did not question the sincerity of the apolitical position adopted by the leaders of the AGE of Paris-Science.
4. *Ibid.*
5. Alain Chiffre, *Les Sources du syndicalisme depuis 1945* (Paris: UNEF Centre de Documentation, 1963), III, 192. Also see Chapter 3, p. 31 above.
6. For the full figures, see Chapter 3, note 36.
7. *Ibid.* It is unclear whether 1965 refers to 1964–1965 or 1965–1966.
8. In addition to the brochure on the *allocation d'études* prepared by the FNEF chapter at Paris-Law, see François Broche, "Lepape et Brigitte Bardot," *La France Etudiante* (December 1963–January 1964), p. 12, and *Le Marxisme dans l'Université* prepared by the Service de Polycopiage Universitaire of the FNEF at Grenoble.
9. The reaction of the FNEF to the student revolt of May and June 1968 was interesting. By this time the FNEF's attitude toward the Gaullists had hardened considerably. The organization virulently attacked the

government for its education policies and use of "police violence," while issuing a warning to the students that certain extremist groups were trying to use the revolt for their own purposes and that this would play into the hands of the Gaullists. A large banner informing Gaullists that they were not welcome was suspended across the entire width of the FNEF's national office. And at the National Congress held in July, the FNEF announced that it was abandoning its "sterile policy of apoliticism."

10. Pierre Bourdieu and Jean-Claude Passeron, *Les Etudiants et leurs études* (Paris: Mouton, 1964), p. 31. See Chapter 4, note 23, for the nature of the Bourdieu and Passeron sample.

11. Robert Michels, *Political Parties*, trans. Eden and Cedar Paul (Glencoe: The Free Press, 1958), and David Truman, *The Governmental Press* (New York: Alfred A. Knopf, 1951), pp. 139–155.

12. Truman, *op. cit.*, pp. 150–151 and 153–154.

13. *Ibid.*, pp. 148–149.

14. Interview with Michel Mousel, 28 May 1964.

15. Jacques Frèyssinet, "Où Vont les Etudiants?" *Cahiers de la République*, V, No. 26 (July–August 1960), 14.

16. Chiffre, *op. cit.*, pp. 236–237.

17. *Ibid.*

18. *Ibid.*

19. They voted not to participate.

20. France has a draft system which combines student deferments with universal military service. A student in good health will receive a deferment only with the assurance that he will serve as soon as he finishes his studies.

21. Michels, *op. cit.*, p. 99.

22. Chiffre, *op. cit.*, Appendix 8.

23. Jacques François Lefèvre, "L'Union Nationale des Etudiants de France depuis 1945" (unpublished thesis submitted at the Institut d'Etudes Politiques, Paris, 1957–1958), p. 32.

24. This interviewee expressed the wish to remain anonymous.

25. Truman, *op. cit.*, pp. 129–139, and Robert A. Dahl and Charles E. Lindblom, *Politics, Economics, and Welfare* (New York: Harper and Row, 1953), pp. 287–294.

26. There were 2,300 signatories, according to Bernard Schreiner, president of UNEF, 1964–1965, interview of 19 July 1964. *Le Monde*, 4 April 1964, reported that there were 2,200 signatories.

27. See "L'Affaire Paris-Science," *21•27: l'Etudiant de France*, Numéro Spécial, 53rd Congress, p. 11.

28. *Ibid.*

29. "Incident devant le petit écran," *Le Monde*, 7 April 1964, p. 9.

30. S. M. Lipset, Martin Trow, and James Coleman, *Union Democracy* (Garden City: Anchor Books, 1962), pp. 50–69 and 464.

31. Nicole Hautmont, *Habitat et vie étudiante* (Paris: Mutuelle Nationale des Etudiants de France, 1963), p. 50. Hautmont infers from the different responses obtained in the same sample to two questions ("Do you belong to a student union?" and "Do you have a student union membership card?") that a certain percentage of students sees the provision of services as the only significant aspect of membership. She also presents a breakdown of the difference in responses by sex, year of study, and faculty. Statistics on the degree of attachment to the organization by faculty would be extremely interesting. However, close examination of Hautmont's data reveals errors which call its reliability into question.

32. The author is active in the local chapter of a prominent academic interest association in which several hundred members pay very substantial membership dues and receive very little in the form of direct benefits. The invariable pattern is for policy to be decided at business meetings by between twelve and thirty attending members.

Chapter 6

The Sociology of UNEF

In the last chapter we were concerned with the number of students attracted into UNEF and the levels of participation among its members. We shall now turn to consideration of the characteristics of these students who have affiliated with UNEF and who have assumed leadership positions.

Affiliation with External Organizations

There are no precise data on student affiliation with French political parties. However, two studies of the political engagement of French students in the 1950's revealed that the established parties made little impression on the populations studied.

In 1954 François Litaudon reported the responses to questionnaires she distributed to Catholic students. Regarding affiliation with political parties, Litaudon wrote:

> Political activists are rare. Fanatics are considered as strange beings. Above all, members of political parties are missing. Signing petitions and demonstrating are the acts which indicate that we believe in [participating in] political life. The political dimension is provided by student syndicalism.[1]

In 1957 Jean Barale conducted a study of the political orientations of students at the Faculties of Letters and Law at the University of Aix-en-Provence. Barale found a deep antiparty sentiment in the majority of the students. He wrote:

On this point we ran up against the individualistic reaction of the intellectual who finds it morally repugnant to belong to a political group. This reaction is accentuated among the students at Aix by a real sentiment of disgust for everything which concerns political parties.[2]

Only 5.2 per cent of the students in Barale's sample actually belonged to a political party. An additional 30 per cent responded that while they were not party members they were "sympathetic" with specific parties. When asked why they did not translate their sympathies into actual membership, 62.5 per cent of the sympathizers responded that they wished to maintain their independence, 24.2 per cent responded that they were too young and ignorant of political life to join, and 13.3 per cent responded that they felt that actual membership might hurt their future careers.[3]

Barale reached the same conclusion as Litaudon: ". . . politics touches the students largely through the channel of syndical life." [4] The AGE at Aix-en-Provence was overwhelmingly majoritaire; nevertheless, 51 per cent of the students who had voted in its elections reported that noncorporate political considerations had determined their choice among the candidates.[5] In other words, the essence of politics mattered greatly, but its established institutions were not trusted.

A more recent survey conducted among students in psychology, sociology, and philosophy at several universities revealed a considerably more favorable attitude toward political parties. Pierre Bourdieu and Jean-Claude Passeron included separate items on party affiliation and sympathy in the questionnaires which they distributed during their 1961–1962 and 1962–1963 surveys. Unfortunately, in the published presentation of their data, the authors reported only the combined percentages of affiliated and sympathetic students. Approximately 47 per cent of the total sample either affiliated with a political party or reported that there was a political party which represented their opinions. Over 50 per cent of the students who had attained majority (twenty-one years of age) either affiliated or sympathized with a political party.[6]

Within the minoritaire movement itself there has been a recent transition in the relations of its militants to the political parties.

From the minoritaire victory in 1956, throughout the Algerian War, and up to 1964, there predominated strains of animosity or indifference toward the political parties. These biases were reflected in an extremely meager representation of members of political parties among UNEF's leaders and in the policy and practice of "intersyndicalism," in accordance with which UNEF sought cooperative action and support from teacher and labor organizations while maintaining a distance from the political parties.[7]

There were several reasons for this estrangement. First, the young people had just been liberated from the authoritarian constraints of the French family and school. They were concerned with maintaining their own personal independence from adult hierarchies and with maintaining the integrity and image of UNEF as a viable independent student organization. Only under these conditions could the organization satisfy the students' need for collective self-assertion.

Second, there existed a political basis as well for disenchantment with the two major political parties of the left, the Communist Party and the SFIO. The slavish adherence of the French Communist Party to the dictates of the Soviet Party, the lack of internal democracy and the extremely tight discipline, the opposition to UNEF's proposal for a system of sustaining scholarships for all students, and the denunciation of UNEF for creating an atmosphere of "confusion and dispersion"[8] during the Algerian War repelled the vast majority of the minoritaires.

The enmity directed toward the SFIO was based almost exclusively upon its support for the Algerian War. The secretary general of the SFIO, Guy Mollet, vigorously prosecuted the war when he headed the government in 1956 and imposed discipline upon the antiwar faction within the party. And Mollet's fellow party member and political ally, Robert Lacoste, was extremely vehement in his denunciation of the antiwar movement during his two years of service as Minister of Algerian Affairs.[9] He is also reported to have urged the government to grant recognition to the Mouvement des Etudiants de France et de l'Union Française pour la Réunification de l'UNEF,[10] which, it will be recalled, was formed by the dissidents within UNEF who walked out of the Congress of 1957.

Third, the inability of the traditional political parties to deal with the Algerian issue and their almost total impotence under the Fifth Republic eliminated a major motive for joining a political party—political efficacy. The opposition parties did not appear to exert any more influence on the policy of the government than did UNEF.[11]

However, from 1964 to the present, students affiliating with political parties have played a progressively more important role in UNEF. Several interacting factors account for this shift. Among them are: the immobilization of UNEF as a viable corporate interest group; the loss of the Algerian issue and the absence of any other noncorporate issue salient enough to mobilize a large number of students who were not already mobilized by those parties; the assertion of independence which the student affiliate of the French Communist Party, the Union des Etudiants Communistes (UEC) made from its parent party; the formation of a new and more attractive party, the Parti Socialiste Unifié (PSU); and the fading of the tradition of the Jeunesse Etudiante Chrétienne (JEC).

Table 6–1 presents data supplied to the author in 1965–1966 by the minoritaire presidents of four provincial AGES, one AGE at a Parisian faculty, and one local organization at a Parisian grande école. The data reveal that 28.4 per cent of the seventy-four minoritaire leaders of these chapters belonged to the student affiliate of either the Communist Party or the PSU and that an additional 9.5 per cent sympathized with them. By the summer of 1967 the major competition within UNEF was between the members and sympathizers of these two parties.

The Communist Party and Offshoot Organizations

Unfortunately, no real data exist on the political affiliations of the early minoritaires. However, since communist and progressive Catholic students are reported to have dominated the Union Patriotique des Organisations d'Etudiants, it is reasonable to assume that some of the early minoritaires did belong to the Communist Party.[12]

More precise information is available on the role played by students affiliated with the Communist Party in the minoritaire movement after 1956. It was in that year that the minoritaires

TABLE 6–1 *Members and Sympathizers of Political Parties Among 74 Minoritaire Leaders of Six AGES (1965–1966)*

	MEMBERS	SYMPATHIZERS	MEMBERS AND SYMPATHIZERS
Parti Socialiste Unifié (PSU)	9 (12.2%)	6 (8.1%)	15 (20.3%)
Communist Party	12 (16.2%)	1 (1.4%)	13 (17.6%)
Section Française de l'Internationale Ouvrière (SFIO)	4 (5.4%)	0 (—)	4 (5.4%)
TOTAL	25 (33.8%)	7 (9.5%)	32 (43.3%)

SOURCE: Responses to questionnaires distributed by the author to AGE presidents during the course of the academic year 1965–1966.

regained control of UNEF and that the Communist Party began a serious campaign to attract students by creating the Union des Etudiants Communistes (UEC).

Despite the poor image of the parent Communist Party in student circles and the serious differences which have arisen between it and UNEF, the Union des Etudiants Communistes has exerted a significant attraction on those minoritaires who have been inclined to affiliate with external organizations. While only four of the seventy-four minoritaire leaders on whom we were supplied data affiliated with the SFIO in 1965–1966, eleven affiliated and one sympathized with the UEC, and one affiliated directly with the parent party. As of the beginning of the academic year 1967–1968, the AGES at the Faculty of Science at Orsay and at eight of the provincial universities were controlled by members of the UEC.[13]

At the national level, members of the UEC were barred from the National Bureau of UNEF during the entire course of the Algerian War. The first member of the UEC to serve on the Bureau was elected by the 1962 Congress, and three more were elected in 1963.[14] Immediately after the confrontations of 1963–1964, this representation was doubled. Six of the fifteen Bureau members elected by the Congress held in April 1964 were members of the UEC.[15] Two of them were also members of the Provisional National

Committee of the UEC, which had been elected one month before UNEF's Congress met.[16] However, at most one member of the UEC has attained the national presidency of UNEF,[17] and, since the Congress of 1966, their members have been deprived of influence on the National Bureau.[18]

Between 1963 and 1965 the UEC was in a state of open rebellion against the parent party. This dispute provides an excellent illustration of the overwhelming strength of the desire for independence from nonstudent hierarchies, even among those students who in fact join organizations with such affiliations.

The 6th UEC Congress, held in February 1963, was characterized by polarization. On one side were the followers of the line of the Central Committee of the adult party. They were called "suivistes" ("followers") or Thorezians, after the late secretary general of the Communist Party, Maurice Thorez.[19] Opposed to the Thorezians, and removing them from control over the UEC, was an alliance of rebellious individuals and factions. Within the new majority the ideological alignments were quite confused.[20]

Between the 6th and 7th Congresses the lines of ideological division among the non-Thorezians became clearer. The dominant faction was referred to by the press as the "Italians," because of their attraction to the theories of the late secretary general of the Italian Communist Party, Palmiro Togliatti. The Central Committee of the party referred to them by the pejorative term communist parlance reserves for right-wing deviationists: "opportunists." Two smaller factions, one Maoist and the other Trotskyist, also emerged. The Central Committee of the party did not differentiate between the two factions and condemned both for Maoist "adventurism" and "leftism." Much to the dismay of the Trotskyists, the French press accepted the classification of the Central Committee and referred to both of these factions as the "Chinese."

At the 7th Congress of the UEC, held in March 1964, the "Italians" emerged as clear victors.[21] They pushed through a program that contained the following essential points: (1) a condemnation of Stalinism, with the implication that the French party was still too Stalinist, (2) a call, inspired by the pronouncements and writings of Togliatti for the development of national forms of communism, a path to socialism as a function of French economic and political conditions, (3) a call for a more open attitude toward noncommunist groups of the left and an announcement that the UEC would participate in a "Student Conference for Democracy and Socialism" with students of the PSU and the SFIO,[22] (4) an assertion of independence from the adult party and of the right to take positions different from those set down by the Central Committee, (5) a call for guarantees of democracy within the UEC and the provision that all points of view be presented in the internal bulletin of the organization and proportionally represented on the deliberative, but not the administrative, organs of the UEC, and (6) a statement of unqualified support for the educational policies of UNEF.[23]

Also, Pierre Kahn, the "Italian" secretary general of the UEC, delivered an address in which he made it clear that, on questions regarding the university and student affairs, the UEC was going to defer to UNEF:

> [The political role of the UEC] is to point out the political dimension of all of the problems and all of the aspirations of the students. . . . This role of the UEC implies, for example, that our aim cannot be to substitute ourselves for the student union, to become the mass organization par excellence which is responsible for formulating the demands and defending the interests of the students. UNEF exists! And its existence, its policies, and its successes must, once and for all, open the eyes of those among us who might think that the UEC should play the same role as UNEF.[24]

During the period of rebellion within the UEC, the influence of the Thorezians in UNEF's politics was minimal. In 1963–1964 the only AGE firmly under the control of the Thorezians was the one at Clermont-Ferrand.[25] And of the six members of the UEC elected to UNEF's National Bureau at the 1964 Congress, only two were Thorezians. The remaining four were "Italians." [26]

Members of the UEC played the leading role in the creation of an extremely radical alliance within UNEF known as the Syndical Left (Gauche Syndicale). The ideas behind this grouping were first visible in Parisian AGES in which there had been militant activity in the antifascist movement during the Algerian War. In particular it emerged out of the minoritaire AGES at the Faculties of Letters (the Sorbonne) and Medicine, literary and scientific preparation, the Ecoles Normales Supérieures, and convalescence homes.[27] But the doctrine received its highest degree of development at the Sorbonne under the leadership of two students, Marc Kravetz and Jean-Louis Peninou. Two elements differentiated this tendency from that of the more moderate minoritaires like Mousel. First, there was a greater emphasis placed upon the noncorporate or environmental role of UNEF. The organization was to serve as the antiregimist vanguard of the working class. Second, there was greater emphasis placed upon direct confrontation with the government, in the manner of the Segni Affair.[28]

Because of their role in the affair, the bids of Kravetz and Peninou to secure positions on the National Bureau were rejected at the 1964 Congress. However, at the General Assembly held the following September they were successful. From that time to the summer of 1966 the Syndical Left dominated the National Bureau. But the leadership was unable to translate the doctrine into any kind of concrete action. The alliance disintegrated into ideologically sectarian groups and its official demise was marked by the election of the Terrel Bureau in the summer of 1966.

All of this dissident activity was, of course, completely unacceptable to the Central Committee of the party. After the UEC's 1964 Congress, the Central Committee attempted to stop the printing of the March–April issue of *Clarté*, the magazine of the UEC: the issue contained an account of the events of the month, the full text of Kahn's speech, and an article by Togliatti. The press of *L'Humanité* was ordered not to print the issue (it also refused to turn over the set plates to the UEC) and pressure was exerted upon a commercial printer who was an important client of the party not to accept the job.[29] The students made public the resistance of the party, appealed to the public for contributions, and managed to publish the issue.

The second tactic which the Central Committee attempted was to merge the UEC with two other communist youth movements which were firmly under the control of followers of the Committee, the Union de la Jeunesse Communiste and the Union des Jeunes Filles de France. The officers of the UEC, though agreeing at least to meet with the leaders of the two other groups, publicly pointed out that the attempt to render the UEC subservient by such organizational maneuvering was a nice example of "Stalinist bureaucratization." [30]

During the months of May and June the leaders of the UEC were subjected to an intense barrage of verbal attacks from supporters of the Central Committee and even from the new secretary general of the party, Waldeck Rochet. Speaking before the 17th Congress of the French Communist Party, he criticized the "opportunism" and "leftism" of the students. He prophesied:

> But, among the students like everywhere else, opportunism and leftism will be defeated because student Communists, who are inspired by the just line of the party to make the UEC a great organization capable of leading the mass of students into battle on the side of the working classes and all the democratic forces, are becoming more and more numerous.[31]

The rather heroic stand of the dissident students in the face of this barrage of criticism gained them a great deal of sympathy and support in intellectual circles. On 9 December 1964, six prominent French writers (Jean-Paul Sartre, Simone de Beauvoir, Yves Berger, Jean-Pierre Faye, Jean Ricardo, and Jorge Semprun) discussed "Que peut la Littérature?" before an overflow crowd at the Mutualité. The proceeds from the admission tickets went to the UEC to finance the publication of *Clarté*.

In February 1965 approximately one hundred communist university professors made public a letter which they had sent to the secretary general of the party, Waldeck Rochet. In the letter they asked him to organize a "Study Day of Communist Intellectuals" to examine the problems of the UEC. In his response Waldeck Rochet rejected the letter and informed the academics that they would be subjected to the discipline of their cells, for acting outside the established channels of communication provided by the party and for supporting a group engaged "in open battle with the party." He went on to express bitter resentment over the support which the students had received outside the party:

> Today, certain leaders of the UEC have come to attack the party, its policies, its principles, and its militants openly and publicly. They

are benefitting from exterior support. All of this is [designed] to turn the UEC into an organization oriented against the party and its policies.[32]

The Central Committee did not content itself with words, however. Through a combination of financial pressure, expulsions, and the strengthening of obedient chapters in the provinces, the Central Committee managed to reassert its control over the UEC in 1965.[33]

After the "Italians" lost their majority at the UEC's March Congress, most either left the organization or were expelled. They did not form another organization. The next to leave were important members of the Syndical Left and Trotskyists. This was accomplished in October 1965, by dissolving the UEC chapter at the Sorbonne and creating a new one under the control of the Central Committee. In March 1967 the less rigid and doctrinaire "Frankist" Trotskyist students formed the Jeunesse Communiste Révolutionnaire (JCR), an organization centered at the Sorbonne and not affiliated with any political party. The students who adhered to the more doctrinaire and disciplined "Lambertist" brand of Trotskyism were already covertly members of the Comité de Liaison des Etudiants Révolutionnaires (CLER), the student affiliate of the tiny Parti Communiste Internationaliste.[34] The Maoists were the last to go. They were expelled early in 1966. The Maoist students, again largely Parisian, created the Union des Jeunesses Communistes (Marxiste–Leniniste) (UJCML).[35] This organization antedates and is totally independent of the pro-Chinese Parti Communiste Révolutionnaire (Marxiste–Leniniste).

Neither the pro-Chinese nor the Trotskyists have been successful within UNEF. Though the president elected in 1966, M. Terrel, turned out to be Maoist, he either did not reveal his orientation before his election or developed it during his term of office. Most of the delegates at the Congress were under the impression that they were electing a more moderate bureau than the previous one controlled by the Syndical Left. When it became clear that Terrel had a Maoist orientation he was forced to resign halfway through his term. And while students belonging to the UEC controlled nine AGES at the beginning of the academic year 1967–1968, pro-Chinese students controlled only one chapter (the Ecole Normale

Supérieure in Paris) and students in the CLER only two provincial chapters (Besançon and Clermont–Ferrand). No AGE was under the control of students belonging to the JCR.[36]

Despite the fact that the Central Committee reasserted its control over the UEC in 1965 and purged the major dissident elements from its ranks shortly thereafter, "mopping up" operations—that is, the dissolution of chapters and the expulsion of students for deviationism—continued throughout the academic year 1966–1967.[37] While the Central Committee has been successful in bringing the student organization back into line, at least for the short term, the UEC certainly has not proved to be the smooth and effective instrument for the recruitment of students into the parent party which had been anticipated when it was created. It is doubtful that a high percentage of the students who have affiliated with the UEC since 1962 have transferred their allegiance to the parent party. In January 1967 four former national leaders of the UEC who had become regular party members after their student years resigned and publicly accused the Central Committee of renouncing the revolutionary vocation and of suppressing dissent within both the parent party and the UEC.[38]

The major attraction of the Communist Party in student circles has been its revolutionary heritage and its strong commitment to social and economic equality. Because of these attributes and the persistent elements of inequalitarianism in French society, the party will continue to exert a certain attraction on idealistic and rebellious students. But, so long as it maintains a separate student affiliate only to impose a strict system of discipline on it, the party is going to continue to be plagued by manifestations of independence on the part of its student members. It is extremely interesting that the student affiliate is the only one of the three youth affiliates of the Communist Party to present such a problem.[39]

The Parti Socialiste Unifié (PSU)

The Parti Socialiste Unifié (PSU) was the result of a merger, in 1960, of the Parti Socialiste Autonome (PSA) and the Union de la Gauche Socialiste (UGS). The PSA was created by a dissident faction of the SFIO after the latter's 1958 Congress. The faction left the SFIO because of the party's support of the Algerian War and the rather brusque treatment accorded to the opponents of the war by the leadership. The UGS was also formed in 1958, primarily of individuals who had left the Communist Party or the Catholic MRP over the war issue. The merger of the PSA and the UGS was thus a logical one. It resulted in the creation of a party with approximately 16,000 card-carrying members.[40]

Since its creation the PSU has been the only noncommunist party to attract a significant number of those minoritaires with external political affiliations. In 1965–1966 nine of the seventy-four minoritaire leaders on whom we were supplied data belonged to the student affiliate of the PSU, the Etudiants Socialistes Unifiés (ESU),[41] and six additional leaders sympathized with them. And, though only one member of the National Bureau elected at UNEF's 1964 Congress belonged to the PSU,[42] members of and sympathizers with the party have controlled the National Bureau since the ouster of the Terrel group at the General Assembly of January 1967. Their support is entirely provincial. At the Congress of 1967, thirteen provincial AGES were controlled by members of the PSU or those sympathetic enough to throw their support to the ultimately victorious, PSU-dominated list of candidates for national office.[43]

A fact of great importance is that the party affords some minoritaire leaders a channel for participation in politics after their student years. The following items were included in the questionnaire distributed to AGE presidents in 1965–1966: "Do you wish to participate in political life after you have finished your studies? How? With which political groups?" Of the seven minoritaire presidents who responded to these items, two said they were not certain that they wanted to participate in the future and five said they did want to participate. Of the latter five, three definitely and one "probably" expected to work within the PSU, and one expected to participate in the communist-dominated labor union, the Conféd-ération Générale du Travail. The PSU was thus the only political party considered acceptable for future political engagement by any of the respondents. Moreover, of the fourteen minoritaire national presidents of UNEF between 1956 and 1968, at least half affiliated with the PSU either during or subsequent to their tenure.

Several attributes of the PSU render it attractive to the minoritaires. First, the party came into existence as a protest against the same policies and tactics of the established parties which had alienated the minoritaires. Second, the party is extremely tolerant of diverse viewpoints and encompasses people with diverse political backgrounds and perspectives. In this regard, it is quite similar to the minoritaire movement itself. Third, the intellectual level of the membership and leadership is extremely high. Almost 25 per cent of the members of the organization were engaged in the teaching profession at some level in 1962.[44] The ex-secretary general of the party, Georges Depreux, held the degree of *agrégation,* was a former professor and Minister of Education (1948), and was always a strong supporter of UNEF. Fourth, the presence of Pierre Mendès-France in the PSU has been of inestimable advantage in recruiting students. Over a decade after he served as premier, he was still undoubtedly the single most attractive figure to students on the left side of the political spectrum. Fifth, the PSU has not "dirtied its hands": it is not a party of the Fourth Republic and it has not had to face the stresses which accompany political power at the national level.

The Jeunesse Etudiante Chrétienne and the Jeunesse Universitaire Chrétienne

In a thesis written in 1958 Jacques François Lefèvre states: "The *jécistes* [students in the Jeunesse Etudiante Chrétienne, JEC] constitute a good part of the leadership of the minoritaire faction of UNEF. They have given this faction a somewhat idealistic character." [45]

At the national level, progressive Catholic students who have been members of the JEC or who have considered themselves of JEC "inspiration" held a virtual monopoly on the presidency of UNEF from 1956 to 1965. In 1964–1965 three members of the National Bureau, including the president, were of JEC "inspiration." [46] And eighteen of the seventy-four officers of our six minoritaire locals were reported by their presidents to have had an ideological preference for, or membership in, the JEC or the Jeunesse Universitaire Chrétienne (JUC) in 1965–1966.

To a great extent, the success which progressive Catholic students have had in gaining leadership positions within UNEF was due to their experience in the Catholic scouting movement. There, at an early age, they became accustomed to group interaction, to leadership responsibility, to the concept of organizing for the performance of functions dictated by a sense of social responsibility. Thus, many of these students were prepared to engage themselves in syndical activity as soon as they entered institutions of higher education. And, as was explained in the last chapter, anyone who wishes to attain a national office in UNEF must begin his syndical career early.

Yet very few of the progressive Catholic minoritaire leaders who have served since 1957 have actually been members of the JEC. For the JEC, like the Union des Etudiants Communistes seven years later, was the scene of a violent student reaction to the attempt of a nonstudent hierarchy to impose policy and discipline from above. In this case the hierarchy was that of the Catholic Church.

Aside from UNEF, the JEC is the oldest student organization in France. Its roots go back to the formation of the Association Catholique de la Jeunesse Française (ACJF) by Count Albert de Mun in 1886. Marc Jussieu describes this early organization as being in the "rural aristocratic tradition of social christianity." [47]

The ACJF was a unitary structure, grouping young people from all walks of life. After World War I, however, the young workers in the movement exerted pressure for the creation of a suborganization of their own. In 1927 the first functional subgroup, the Jeunesse Ouvrière Chrétienne (JOC), was created. Before long the ACJF was divided into five subgroups, of workers, farmers, sailors and fishermen, students, and "independents." The student group, the Jeunesse Etudiante Chrétienne, was created in 1929.[48]

The crisis in the modern movement developed from a disagreement which arose between the leaders of the JEC and the JOC (workers) in 1954. It was not political in content, for both subgroups were dominated by Christian socialists who refused to admit a separation between the socio-political and religious realms. Their ideology was inspired by the social gospel of Christ, which, they claimed, taught that social and political action was an integral part of "Catholic action."

The disagreement was over the relative power that the functional subgroups should exercise within the ACJF. The leaders of the workers' group wanted to turn the parent organization into a forum where the leaders of the subgroups could meet and discuss issues but where a common position could be taken only by unanimous agreement. The student leaders opposed this. They feared that such a divided structure would result in the isolation of the students from the other segments of progressive Catholic youth. The ACJF split over the issue into two antagonistic camps, and the split spread to the lower clerics. In September 1956 André Vial, the young farmer who had been president of the ACJF for two and a half years and who had attempted to resolve the dispute, resigned in desperation.[49]

In November the Church hierarchy decided to resolve the issue from above. The Assembly of Cardinals and Archbishops issued a doctrinal paper which was intended to clarify the purposes of the youth movement. Ironically, while it supported the position of the students on the organizational issue, the paper threw the JEC into a state of crisis.

The paper drew a distinction between "social and civic action" and "Catholic action," and stated that the same organization should not attempt to engage in both. The paper maintained that the ACJF was an organization for "Catholic action." Therefore, it continued, "it is natural that those who do not have the faith or have a vacillating faith see the relationship between the laity and the hierarchy only in a human, and often a political, perspective." [50]

The leadership of the JEC, which was extremely concerned with the Algerian War, did not accept the paper with equanimity. A letter disputing the distinction between the two types of action was sent by the general secretariat to all secretaries of local chapters.[51] Six months later the JEC was shattered by the resignations, en masse, of eighty top leaders of the movement. This coincided with the resignation of the entire national board of *La Route*, the senior branch of the Catholic scouting movement. The immediate stimulus for their resignation was the refusal of the hierarchy to allow *La Route* to publish the letters of a former national board member who had been killed in Algeria. The letters, which were to have been published in the magazine of the movement, were critical of certain forms of "pacification" being practiced by the French in Algeria.[52]

Since the Catholic party, the Mouvement Républicain Populaire (MRP), contained a strongly rightist and *Algérie française* element, progressive Catholic students had only one other place to engage themselves, UNEF.[53] However, most of the progressive Catholic students within the minoritaire movement have maintained a symbolic bond with the leaders of the JEC who resigned in 1957 by continuing to refer to themselves as *jécistes* or of JEC "inspiration." Between 1957 and 1965 no autonomous progressive Catholic organization existed for students. Some of these students joined the PSU after its formation in 1960, but the longing for a vital independent Catholic alternative to the JEC remained. During the academic year 1964–1965 the leadership of the sorely weakened JEC once again found itself in conflict with the church hierarchy because of its stands.

While the dispute again involved general interpretation of "Catholic action," three specific policy positions adopted by the leadership of the JEC had severely provoked the hierarchy. First, the students took the position that the French educational system was painfully inequalitarian because a capitalist society was incapable of producing any other kind. Second, the students voiced strong opposition to the Fouchet Reforms. And, third, they criticized the church hierarchy for not facing squarely up to the injustices and iniquities in French society; furthermore, they maintained that it was up to the laity to prod the Church.[54] On the first two issues the position of the leadership of the JEC was identical with that of UNEF.

This dispute dealt the coup de grâce to the JEC in university circles. As of 1967–1968 its national leaders were all university students, but its recruitment was almost exclusively limited to students in institutions of secondary and vocational education.[55]

Two subsequent attempts have been made to create organizations which would replace the JEC. Neither has been successful. During the academic year 1965–1966 dissidents from the JEC and progressive Catholic students who had refused to participate in the JEC came together to form a group independent of the church hierarchy, the Jeunesse Universitaire Chrétienne (JUC). Two years after its formation the organization is virtually nonexistent. Another organization, created in July 1966, is the Action Catholique Universitaire (ACU). This organization is related to the hierarchy and is much more timid about taking specific political positions than was the JUC. In Paris it is controlled by the Mission Etudiante, which is under the sponsorship of the hierarchy. And the ACU receives funds from, and publishes a common newspaper with, the JEC. The ACU is, however, very small and does not even bother with the formality of elections to choose its national leaders.

Area of Study

In France there is apparently no correlation between the different academic disciplines and student activism as such. However, Alain Chiffre maintains that there is a significant correlation between one's academic discipline and minoritaire versus corporatist orientations. Chiffre contends that students in letters and science tend to be attracted to the minoritaire movement more than do students in professional schools while the latter tend to be attracted to corporatism more than do the former.[56]

A priori, such a correlation would seem to make sense. Students in professional schools are more concretely future-oriented than are students in letters and science. They are certain of their future professional roles and tend to identify in rather immediate, specific terms with them. Student experience they tend to view in a highly utilitarian perspective: it is a time when one learns his trade. On the other hand, students in letters and science are less certain of their future roles in society, so for them the student experience takes on a much greater intrinsic meaning: it becomes a highly significant stage in the intellectual and psychological development of the self. While the minoritaires have defined the student in terms of a present condition (a "young, intellectual worker"), the FNEF has stressed the future dimension ("free student, future cadre of a free society").

Further, students in professional schools tend to be more conservative politically than are students in letters and science.[57] And the minoritaire movement is a movement of the political left. Students in professional schools more than students in letters and science tend to feel that they have a vested interest in the maintenance of the status quo. They fear that political change in a socialist direction will cause them economic deprivation by destroying the traditional patterns of private interaction in their professions. Thus the FNEF, which claims to be apolitical, is really a defender of the status quo, a proponent of the preservation of a liberal capitalist society. Students in letters and science, on the other hand, are more likely to orient themselves toward work in the public sector (for example, education and research), which the advent of socialism would not change.[58] Moreover, by the very nature of their choice of discipline and in accord with the content of their studies, students in letters and science are more oriented toward abstract patterns of thought and morality than are students in professional schools, with the possible exception of law students. They are more inclined to identify themselves as intellectuals and to play the traditional role of the intellectual.[59]

Finally, while it is true that French medical students have shown dissatisfaction with their program of studies and the nature of their profession, it is the students in letters and science, particularly the former, who have been the hardest hit by overcrowding, by inadequate working facilities, and by unemployment. And it was our contention in Chapter 4 that these problems are conducive to a sense of identity and solidarity qua students and to a propensity to think in terms of radical systemic changes.

The quantitative data which this writer has been able to gather tend to support Chiffre's contention that there is a positive correlation between the minoritaire orientation and enrollment in a faculty of letters or science and between the corporatist orientation and enrollment in a professional school. They support this contention, however, with two qualifications. First, at the national level the most important sources of leaders for the minoritaire movement have been the faculties of letters and the Institut d'Etudes Politiques in Paris; the contribution of the faculties of science has not been impressive. Second, geography is an intervening variable; the correlation seems to hold in the provinces but not in Paris.

At the national leadership level, of the fourteen minoritaire presidents of UNEF who served between 1946 and 1965, five were students in letters, four at the Institut d'Etudes Politiques in Paris, two in law, one in science, one in dentistry, and one in a technical school. On the other hand, of the eight majoritaire presidents of UNEF who served from November 1950 to July 1956, four were medical students, two were students in letters, one in dentistry, and one in law. Of the first four national presidents of the Fédération Nationale des Etudiants de France, an organization created by dissident elements within the professional and commercial *offices* of UNEF, two were law students, one (the first president) a medical student, and one a dentistry student.[60]

Because provincial AGES group together students in all faculties and institutions connected with their universities, the provincial membership figures possessed by the national office of UNEF are not broken down by academic discipline, as are the Parisian ones. Only four presidents of provincial chapters—who returned the questionnaires in 1965–1966—supplied utilizable information regarding the disciplines of their bureau members, and only three supplied such figures for their entire chapters. However, these limited data are consistent with Chiffre's contention, with Barale's findings at the Faculties of Law and Letters at Aix-en-Provence, and with what we know about the history of dissension within the student movement.

Of a total of forty-two officers in the four minoritaire AGES, nineteen were students in letters, fifteen in science, three in law, one each in medicine, pharmacy, and a technical school, and two in university preparatory curricula. Of the combined membership of 2,450 in the three minoritaire chapters for which data were supplied, 49 per cent was composed of science students, 34.6 per cent of students in letters, 6.2 per cent of law students, 5.3 per cent of students in medicine or related fields, 3.3 per cent of students in technical schools, and 1.6 per cent of students in preparatory curricula. At one provincial university in which 27.6 per cent of the student body was enrolled in professional schools in 1962–1963, the AGE claimed approximately 1,000 members in the faculties of letters and science and only 130 members in the professional schools.[61] More students in the professional schools affiliated with the Fédération Nationale des Etudiants de France than with UNEF.

While the correlation between enrollment in professional or nonprofessional faculties and corporatist versus minoritaire orientation is very high in the provinces, it does not hold at all in Paris. Table 6–2 ranks the five Parisian faculties according to the per-

TABLE 6–2 *Ranking of the Five Parisian* Facultés *According to the Percentage of the Student Body Therein Affiliating with* UNEF *(1962–1963)*

FACULTÉ	SIZE OF STUDENT BODY	NUMBER OF STUDENTS AFFILIATING WITH UNEF	PERCENTAGE OF STUDENTS AFFILIATING WITH UNEF
Pharmacy	2,799	1,505 (6.4%)	53.7
Medicine	13,672	6,125 (25.9%)	44.8
Science	24,362	8,000 (33.9%)	32.8
Letters	27,513	7,001 (29.6%)	25.4
Law	18,081	1,001 (4.2%)	5.5
TOTAL	86,427	23,632 (100.0%)	27.3

SOURCE: Computed by the author from UNEF membership lists and statistics from the *Bureau de Prévision et de la Documentation, Directeur de l'Enseignement Supérieur, Ministère de l'Education National,* as reported in UNEF—*Informations: Données Statistiques, 53ᵉ Congrès* (Toulouse, 1964).

centage of the student body therein affiliating with UNEF in 1962–1963. The highest rates of recruitment were maintained by the Faculties of Medicine and Pharmacy, both under minoritaire control. The Faculty of Medicine, where corporatists took over the AGE in 1964–1965, has ranked with the Faculty of Letters and the Ecole Normale Supérieure in radical and militant political activism. On the other hand, the AGE at the Faculty of Science, which is the largest chapter in UNEF, has traditionally been the standard bearer of corporatism within the organization. Although there is some tentative indication that the membership's sense of identification with the AGE was higher at the Faculty of Letters than at any other Parisian faculty,[62] the recruitment performance of this minoritaire AGE was far inferior to that of the minoritaire chapters at the Faculties of Pharmacy and Medicine. Only UNEF's poor recruitment at the Faculty of Law, the only one of the five Parisian faculties in which the FNEF had made any headway, was consistent with Chiffre's correlation.

TABLE 6–3 *Participation in* UNEF: *Paris and the Provinces*

CONGRESS	APPROXIMATE PERCENTAGE OF TOTAL STUDENT BODY AFFILIATED WITH UNEF	APPROXIMATE PERCENTAGE OF PARISIAN STUDENT BODY AFFILIATED WITH UNEF	APPROXIMATE PERCENTAGE OF PROVINCIAL STUDENT BODY AFFILIATED WITH UNEF
1945	20	9	31
1950	25	13	36
1957	42	35	47
1963	26	31	23

SOURCE: Percentages for the years 1945, 1950, and 1957 were computed by the author from data presented in Jacques François Lefèvre, "L'Union Nationale des Etudiants de France depuis 1945" (unpublished thesis, Institut d'Etudes Politiques, Paris, 1957–1958), pp. 26–27. Percentages for 1963 were computed by the author from data in UNEF's official 1962–1963 membership files and in UNEF—*Informations, Données Statistiques, 53ᵉ Congrès* (Toulouse, 1964). The total number of all students registered in the student insurance programs was used in these calculations. To obtain an approximate percentage of members among only those students who were enrolled in faculties and grandes écoles, 4 per cent should be added to the percentages in the table.

Geography

Table 6–3 compares the recruitment performance of UNEF in Paris and in the provinces. Until the Algerian issue arose, UNEF's performance had been considerably better in the provinces than in the capital: this was true under both minoritaire and corporatist national leadership. However, its position on the Algerian issue cost UNEF much more dearly in the provinces than in Paris. During 1962–1963, the academic year which followed the termination of the Algerian War, the percentage of students recruited into provincial AGES was lower than at any time since the end of World War II and approximately half of what it had been in 1956–1957. The decrease in the rate of recruitment in Paris was, on the other hand, only slight.

Two points should be made regarding the Paris-province dichotomy. First, UNEF's maintenance of a relatively high rate of recruitment in Paris was undoubtedly helped by the politicalized life of the capital and by the difficult working and living conditions which exist there. But it was also due to the tenacity and loyalty of majoritaire activists in some Parisian AGES. With the exception of those at the Faculty of Law, they showed little inclination to quit UNEF and join the government-supported FNEF, unlike their provincial counterparts. Thus while all of the provincial AGES were under solid minoritaire control in 1962–1963 and 1963–1964, the giant AGE of Paris-Science was under majoritaire control, and the minoritaires faced stiff internal opposition in several other Parisian chapters. As was indicated above, the majoritaires have made two major gains since the immobilization of UNEF in 1963–1964, with victories in the Parisian AGES at the Faculty of Medicine and the Institut d'Etudes Politiques.

Second, the particular geographical location is a more precise variable than the simple Paris-province dichotomy. While in 1962–1963 Paris contained 35 per cent of the total French student body and an impressive 42 per cent of UNEF's total membership, Table 6–4 indicates that the organization enjoyed an even higher rate of recruitment in four provincial academic districts: Reims, Dijon, Lille-Amiens, and Besançon. The table also indicates that the greatest successes in recruiting have been in the extreme north and northeast of the country, while the poorest performances have been in the extreme south and southwest. The only universities in which the local affiliates of the Fédération Nationale des Etudiants de France were stronger than those of UNEF were located in the Midi (southern coastal region). They were Aix-en-Provence, Avignon, Nice, and Toulon. The only university in which UNEF did not have any AGE was Montpellier, also located in the Midi.[63] It was in the Faculty of Medicine of this university that the idea for the creation of the FNEF was born. Thus, with the exception of that traditional minoritaire stronghold of the south, Toulouse, the split over Algeria has been disturbingly costly in this generally conservative region with deep *Algérie française* sentiments.

Sex

At the level of simple membership, the rate of participation in UNEF is approximately the same among male and female students. In their 1961–1962 and 1962–1963 surveys, Bourdieu and Pas-

TABLE 6–4 *Ranking of French Academic Districts According to the Percentage of the Student Body Therein Affiliating with* UNEF *(1962–1963)*

ACADÉMIE	SIZE OF STUDENT BODY	NUMBER OF STUDENTS AFFILIATING WITH UNEF	PERCENTAGE OF STUDENTS AFFILIATING WITH UNEF
Reims	2,648	1,218	46.0
Dijon	5,547	2,201	39.7
Lille, Amiens	18,141	6,701	36.9
Besançon	4,450	1,501	33.7
Paris	115,061	35,898	31.2
Poitiers, Limoges	7,572	2,302	30.4
Lyon, Saint-Etienne	19,903	6,000	30.1
Toulouse	19,476	5,601	28.8
Grenoble	13,261	3,675	27.7
Nantes, Angers	8,805	2,212	25.1
Rennes, Brest	11,717	2,857	24.4
Strasbourg, Metz, Mulhouse	14,381	3,500	24.3
Clermont	7,153	1,601	22.3
Caen, Rouen	11,100	2,151	19.4
Nancy	10,685	2,000	18.7
Orleans, Tours, Stanford	3,143	500	15.9
Bordeaux, Pau	16,350	2,307	14.1
Aix-Marseille, Nice	22,042	3,007	13.6
Montpellier, Perpignan	16,095	0	—
TOTAL	327,530	85,232	26.0

SOURCE: Computed by the author from UNEF membership lists and statistics from the Centre National des Oeuvres as reported in UNEF—*Informations: Données Statistiques, 53ᵉ Congrès* (Toulouse, 1964). The figures of the *Centre National des Oeuvres* include all students registered in the student insurance program. If we were to limit our consideration to students registered in the faculties and grandes écoles, the total rate of participation would rise to approximately 30 per cent.

seron found that 37 per cent of their male sample affiliated with UNEF, 2 per cent with the FNEF, 3 per cent with one of the three major labor confederations, and 13 per cent with local independent student associations. Of the female sample, 37 per cent affiliated with UNEF, 1 per cent with the FNEF, 1 per cent with one of the three major labor confederations, and 3 per cent with local independent student associations.[64]

The variable of sex does become significant, however, at the leadership level. In the Bourdieu and Passeron survey, 23 per cent of the male sample and 7 per cent of the female sample indicated that they held leadership positions in some interest association.[65] Five presidents of AGES at coeducational institutions (one in Paris and four in the provinces) who responded to our questionnaire supplied data on the sex of their bureau members in 1965–1966. The student population at these institutions was distributed almost evenly between males and females. However, of the 65 Bureau members in these five locals, 49 (75.4 per cent) were males and 16 (24.7 per cent) were females. Thus, the propensity to assume leadership positions in UNEF appears to be approximately three times greater among males than among females.

Age

The Bourdieu and Passeron survey included items on age, social class, and type of residence. Though these variables were not correlated with participation in UNEF, they were correlated with participation in all of the associations mentioned above, that is, UNEF, the FNEF, local independent student associations, and labor unions. Since a large majority of those who participated did so in UNEF, and since the data are unique, we shall report these findings.

Age is not a very significant variable when correlated with membership. Fifty-seven per cent of the sample under twenty-one years of age, 53 per cent between twenty-one and twenty-five years of age, and 62 per cent over twenty-five years of age affiliated with an interest association. As one would expect, however, the percentage of leaders increases with increasing age. Twelve and one-half per cent of the sample under twenty-one years of age, 16 per cent between twenty-one and twenty-five years of age, and 27 per cent over twenty-five years of age held leadership positions.[66] As was pointed out in the last chapter, it takes time to acquire leadership positions and the price paid for assuming such responsibility is often a prolongation of the student career.

Social Class

Students from lower-class backgrounds tend to affiliate with interest associations more than students from middle- and upper-class backgrounds. Seventy-one per cent of the sample from families in which the father was a worker, a farmer, a low ranking civil servant, or a lower echelon nonmanual employee affiliated. Fifty per cent of the sample from families in which the father was the owner of a business, a manager, a high or middle echelon civil servant, or engaged in the liberal professions affiliated. At the leadership level, however, the difference tends to disappear. Eighteen per cent of the sample in the first category and 16 per cent in the second category were leaders.[67]

Since there is only a small percentage of lower-class students in French universities, this means that a small minority of the leaders come from lower-class backgrounds. As we have pointed out, the economic pressures upon the lower-class student make it very difficult for him to assume leadership responsibilities. According to Michel Mousel, president of UNEF in 1963–1964, the tone of UNEF at the leadership level is very distinctly set by students from bourgeois families.[68]

Type of Residence

In the Bordieu and Passeron survey, students living in university housing showed the greatest tendency to belong to interest associations. Students living in private rented lodgings were in the intermediate position, and students living with their parents showed the lowest tendency. Fifty-three per cent of the sampled students living at home, 60 per cent of the students living in private rented quarters, and 83 per cent of the students living in university housing affiliated with an interest association.[69] Students living in university housing have a greater feeling of independence and greater freedom of action than students living with their families. They also live in an environment which is more conducive to intercommunication and interaction with other students than that of either students who live with their parents or in private rented quarters.

NOTES

1. François Litaudon, "Résponses à un questionnaire," in *Recherches et Débats du Centre Catholique des Intellectuels Français*, No. 8, *La France, Va-t-elle Perdre Sa Jeunesse?* (Paris: Librarie Artheme Fayard, July 1954), p. 156.
2. Jean Barale, "Les Etudiants d'Aix-en-Provence et la politique en Mai 1957," *Revue Française de Science Politique*, IX, No. 4 (December 1959), 975.
3. *Ibid.*, p. 979. Percentages computed by this writer from absolute numbers.
4. *Ibid.*, p. 969.
5. *Ibid.*
6. Pierre Bourdieu and Jean-Claude Passeron, *Les Etudiants et leurs études* (Paris: Mouton, 1964), p. 18. Almost all of the students in the sample were drawn from the faculties of letters in the Universities of Bordeaux, Lille, Lyon, Paris, Rennes-Nantes, and Toulouse.
7. As we have seen in Chapter 3, part of this support has taken the form of loans when UNEF has been deprived of its subsidy by the government. As of July 1964 the major creditors of UNEF were the Fédération de l'Education Nationale, the Syndicat National des Instituteurs (the FEN's largest and most powerful affiliate), the Confédération Générale du Travail, and the Ligue Française de l'Enseignement. Interview with Bernard Schreiner, president of UNEF, 19 July 1964.
8. Alain Chiffre, *Les Sources du syndicalisme depuis 1945* (Paris: UNEF Centre de Documentation, 1963), II, 257. The attacks were delivered by Maurice Thorez, the secretary general of the party.
9. Lacoste is credited with having made the following remarks in a speech to a group of war veterans in Algiers: "The exhibitionists of the heart and mind who are conducting the campaign against torture are responsible for the resurgence of terrorism which has resulted in twenty dead and one hundred and fifty wounded in Algiers during the past several days. I consecrate them to your disdain." Cited in Louis Bodin, *Les Intellectuels* (Paris: Presses Universitaires de France, 1962), p. 57. The split within the SFIO during the Algerian War bears some striking similarities to the split which later developed in the American Democratic Party over the Vietnamese War.
10. Chiffre, *op. cit.*, p. 206.
11. While the call of the Gaullist UNR to the students is "Be Effective, Join the Young Gaullists!" it is doubtful that even the UNR is a serious

instrument in the creation of policy. General de Gaulle, who denies that it is a "political party," treats it as a passive support structure.

12. See Chapter 3 of this work.

13. Data courtesy of Jacques Sauvageot, vice-president of UNEF, interview of 20 June 1968.

14. Frank A. Pinner, "Transition and Transgression: Some Characteristics of Student Movements in Western Europe" (unpublished paper presented at the Conference on Students and Politics, San Juan, Puerto Rico, 27–31 March 1967).

15. Interview with Bernard Schreiner, president of UNEF 1964–1965, 19 July 1964.

16. This information was obtained by comparing the published lists of the names of the officers of the two organizations.

17. Acquaintances of President Terrel (summer 1966 to January 1967) inform us that he had been in the UEC, at least prior to his election as the leader of UNEF. Since he was a Maoist and since the Maoists were purged from the UEC in February 1966, it is doubtful that he retained his membership in the UEC during his presidential term in UNEF. Moreover, when his Maoist orientation became clear he was forced to resign from the presidency halfway through his normal term.

18. On the Congress of 1966, see *Le Monde Séléction Hebdomadaire,* 21–27 April 1966, p. 7.

19. Thorez died in 1964.

20. I should like to express my appreciation to M. Frédéric Bon of the Fondation Nationale des Sciences Politiques for his very kind assistance concerning the UEC.

21. The strength of the factions on the Provisional National Committee elected by the Congress was as follows: 35 "Italians," 35 Thorezians, and 13 Maoists and Trotskyists. Approximately one week later, however, this committee elected an overwhelmingly "Italian" National Bureau. See *Le Monde,* 10 March 1964, p. 16, and 18 March 1964, p. 8.

22. UNEF sent a guest delegation and the Fédération Française des Associations Chrétiennes sent an observer delegation. The Conference took place at a time when the relations between the three parties of the left were particularly strained.

23. *Le Monde,* 18 March 1964, p. 8.

24. Pierre Kahn, "Approfondir et Appliquer la Ligne du XXe Congrès," *Clarté,* No. 55 (March–April 1964), p. 7.

25. Interview with Michel Mousel, president of UNEF 1963–1964, 19 May 1964.

26. Interview with Bernard Schreiner, president of UNEF 1964–1965, 19 July 1964.

27. See Alain Chiffre, *op. cit.,* p. 337.

28. For a presentation of the theoretical position of the Syndical Left by one of its leaders see: Marc Kravetz, "Naissance d'un syndicalisme

étudiant," *Les Temps Modernes*, XIX, No. 213 (February 1964), 1447–1475; and Antoine Griset and Marc Kravetz, "De l'Algerie à la Réforme Fouchet: critique du syndicalisme étudiant," *Les Temps Modernes*, XX, No. 227 (April 1965), 1880–1902, and XX, No. 228 (May 1965), 2066–2089. Some of the leaders of the student insurance program, the MNEF, still claim to adhere to the Syndical Left doctrine. Their activities, however, are exclusively research and service.

29. *Le Monde*, 14 May 1964, p. 9.

30. *France-Observateur*, 28 May 1964, p. 4.

31. *Le Monde*, 9 June 1964, p. 7.

32. *Le Monde Sélection Hebdomadaire*, 18–24 February 1965, p. 2.

33. The leaders of the "Italian," Maoist, and "Chinese" factions were largely Parisian students. We were able to obtain data on the institutional affiliations of 22 out of the 24 members of the National Bureau of the UEC elected in March 1964. Seventeen were enrolled in Parisian institutions while only 5 were enrolled in provincial universities. The institutional affiliations were as follows: 5 from Paris-Letters (the Sorbonne), 4 from Paris-Medicine, 2 from the Ecole Normale Supérieure, 2 from Paris-Arts, 2 from other Parisian grandes écoles, 1 from the Faculty of Science at Orsay (a suburb of Paris), 1 from a *lycée* in Paris (*propédeutique*), and one from each of the following provincial universities—Aix-en-Provence, Bordeaux, Montpellier, Toulouse, and Nancy.

34. In April 1968 the name of the CLER, which had been formed in 1961, was changed to the Fédération des Etudiants Révolutionnaires (FER). Both the FER and the JCR were declared to be illegal after the uprising of May and June 1968. The JCR retained its name, but the FER changed its name to the Comité pour la Défense de l'UNEF.

35. The UJCML was also declared to be illegal.

36. Data courtesy of Jacques Sauvageot, vice-president of UNEF, interview of 20 June 1968. It should be pointed out that these organizations are quite small. In 1968 the CLER claimed 1,100 members. The JCR probably had between 1,000 and 1,500. The UJCML probably had something on the order of 2,000 members and sympathizers. A reliable source estimates that in 1964–1965 the UEC had between 2,500 and 3,500 members. While there was some replenishment of the losses due to defections and purges, it probably has not been sufficient to sustain the 1964–1965 membership level. Keith Botsford estimated that approximately 2,000 students belonged to the UEC in 1966–1967. See his "Why Students in France Go Communist: Elite Proletarians All," *New York Times Magazine*, 13 November 1966, pp. 54–99.

37. *Le Monde*, 8–9 January 1967, p. 6.

38. *Ibid.*

39. For a brief treatment of the attraction of the Communist Party among French students, see Botsford, *op. cit.*

40. Membership figure courtesy of M. Klein, former treasurer of the PSU, and M. Claude Bourdet.

41. In an interview of 1 July 1968, M. Jean-Claude Boisseau, a member of the national secretariat of the ESU, estimated that they could claim between 1,000 and 1,200 members. The organization is stronger in the provinces than in Paris.

42. Interview with Bernard Schreiner, president of UNEF 1964–1965, 19 July 1964.

43. Interview with Jacques Sauvageot, vice-president of UNEF, 20 June 1968.

44. Data courtesy of M. Guy Nania.

45. Jacques François Lefèvre, "L'Union Nationale des Etudiants de France depuis 1945" (unpublished thesis submitted at the Institut d'Etudes Politiques, Paris, 1958), p. 34.

46. Interview with Bernard Schreiner, president of UNEF 1964–1965, 19 July 1964.

47. Marc Jussieu, "A.C.J.F.: Signification d'une crise," *Esprit* (January 1956), pp. 116–125.

48. *Ibid.*

49. Marc Jussieu, "A.C.J.F.: Historique d'une démission," *Esprit* (November 1956), pp. 694–696.

50. Marc Jussieu, "Points de repère," *Esprit* (July–August 1957), p. 80.

51. *Ibid.*

52. *Ibid.*, p. 78.

53. The MRP, too, was destroyed by the Algerian issue.

54. See *Le Monde*, 9 April 1965, p. 24; 10 April 1965, p. 11; 11–12 April 1965, p. 14; and 18–19 April 1965, p. 11. The church hierarchy was especially sensitive to this kind of criticism. The Episcopat of Paris had just condemned the progressive Catholic newspaper *Le Témoignage Chrétien* for causing dissension within the Christian community and for dealing with doctrinal and conciliar matters. Thus the dissension between the hierarchy and the JEC was part of a larger conflict between the hierarchy and progressive Catholic intellectuals. Much of this can be traced to the so-called "Dialogues" between Marxist and Christian intellectuals conducted in France.

55. Interview with Jean-Paul Ciret, president of the Jeunesse Etudiante Chrétienne, 3 July 1968.

56. Chiffre, *op. cit.*, p. 280.

57. See Barale, *op. cit.*, pp. 967–968. Comparing a sample of law students with a sample of students in letters at Aix-en-Provence in 1957, Barale comments:

> So long as one looks for physical and even social differences . . . the student milieu appears to be relatively homogeneous. But when one touches upon politics, one really has the impression of being confronted with two opposite groups. To be sure, there are minorities

within each group. Nevertheless, every right wing group or ideology attracts a predominance of law students while the left principally attracts students in letters.

58. Barale (*ibid.*, p. 967) reports that 46 per cent of the law students and 11.5 per cent of the students in letters in his sample of students at Aix-en-Provence expressed a preference to work in the private sector. Of the law students, 37.8 per cent, and of the students in letters, 72.5 per cent, expressed a preference to work in the public sector. Also, see Chapter 4 of this work.

59. In her nonrandom survey of 788 Parisian students in 1961–1962, Nicole Hautmont asked the following question: "Do students already have a role to play in society or should they devote themselves exclusively to their studies?" The breakdown of responses favoring a social role by faculty were as follows: letters 80 per cent, science 77 per cent, law 73 per cent, and medicine 62 per cent. Nicole Hautmont, *Habitat et vie étudiante* (Paris: Mutuelle Nationale des Etudiants de France, 1962), p. 49.

60. See Chiffre, *op. cit.*, Appendix 8.

61. Relations between the AGE and the university administration were particularly poor at this university. Some of the AGE officers maintained that professors in the medical school discouraged participation in UNEF, that some medical students participated secretly, and that some whose participation became known were discriminated against in their grades.

62. See Hautmont, *op. cit.*, pp. 49–52, and Chapter 5, note 31, above.

63. The AGE had split apart due to intense internal conflict; this proved to be temporary.

64. Bourdieu and Passeron, *op. cit.*, 31. On p. 32 they report that 65 per cent of the females affiliated with an interest association while 35 per cent did not. It would appear that the data on p. 31 are the correct data and that the inconsistency between the data on the two pages is the result of a typographical error on p. 32. If the percentages in the "simple member" and "indifferent and hostile" boxes in the table on p. 32 are switched, the data on p. 32 accord with those on p. 31. See Chapter 4, note 23, above, for the nature of the sample.

65. *Ibid.*, p. 32.

66. *Ibid.*, p. 18.

67. *Ibid.*, p. 70.

68. Interview with Michel Mousel, 28 May 1964.

69. Bordieu and Passeron, *op. cit.*, p. 33. In Hautmont's survey students were asked if they participated in a religious, cultural, political, athletic, or student interest groups. The same relative position of students living in the three types of residence was established. See Hautmont, *op. cit.*, pp. 24–25.

Chapter 7

Conclusion: UNEF, the Government, and the Future

French students made an active attempt to influence their environment earlier than did students in most other countries. Almost immediately their initiative was met with societal approval. The most important structure through which French students have articulated their demands has been the Union Nationale des Etudiants de France, the oldest student organization in France and quite possibly the oldest national student organization in existence.

The organization was created in 1907 by the merger of student organizations at several universities. It first began to function as a vigorous interest group during the difficult interwar period. By successfully appealing to both private philanthropic sources and the government, the leaders of UNEF were instrumental in the creation of facilities and services which provide important corporate benefits to French students. The value of the organization was given official recognition in 1929, when UNEF was declared to be of public utility and accorded financial support out of the public treasury.

During the Vichy regime and the Occupation, the leaders of UNEF sought to maintain a corporatist orientation. But this was unsatisfactory to a fascist regime which wanted to use the student group as a vehicle for political mobilization and control. The regime increased its pressure, and UNEF's leaders found themselves maintaining silence in the face of deportations of students to Nazi forced-labor camps, assuring the public powers that the organization was really one of the *ancien régime*, and offering their assistance in the creation of a government-controlled student organization.

In 1946 the supporters of corporatism were voted out of office. With the adoption of the Charter of Grenoble, UNEF was converted into a student- and environment-oriented organization. The authors of the Charter charged that by maintaining silence on political issues during Vichy and the Occupation, the young intellectuals had betrayed their obligation to the nation. They were determined that in the future UNEF, as the institution representing French students, would reflect and encourage a strong sense of civic commitment.

From 1946 to 1950 the organization was led by individuals who shared this commitment. In time, however, the spirit of the Resistance and Liberation faded. Although the Charter of Grenoble was retained, leaders who favored an exclusively corporatist orientation assumed control in 1950. Between 1950 and 1953 they exerted complete control. From 1953 to 1956 they were increasingly forced to admit students favoring a student and environment orientation to the National Bureau as minority coalition partners. In 1956 exponents of a student and environment orientation resumed full control of the organization, again on a specific catalytic issue, the Algerian War. The student and environment orientation is still dominant today.

During the Fourth Republic UNEF maintained its status as a public service organization and regularly received a subsidy from the government. The public powers were even more solicitous of the organization during the Fourth Republic than they had been during the Third Republic. Because of the good relations UNEF's leaders enjoyed with both the Ministry of Education and the powerful Education Committee of the Chamber of Deputies, the student officers sat on several official advisory committees and had an important voice in policy-making on matters of student welfare. Moreover, students were accorded a health insurance program which was administered by their elected representatives. On eight separate occasions during the Fourth Republic, UNEF utilized national strikes and/or demonstrations to publicize and protest what it felt to be insufficient budgetary allocations to higher education. But the channels of access to decision-makers were always kept open, and major victories were obtained through those channels under both corporatist and student- and environment-oriented leadership. By the end of the Fourth Republic UNEF was a vigorous, influential interest association that claimed the voluntary membership of almost half of the nation's university students.

Since the establishment of the Fifth Republic, UNEF has suffered serious setbacks. For the most part, channels of access to governmental decision-makers have been closed. During six of the first nine years of the Fifth Republic, the government has refused to deliver UNEF's subsidy. The appeal of the organization among the national student body has steadily weakened.

UNEF's few victories during the Fifth Republic have been won through adjudication and confrontation. Most have been defensive in nature. Such victories include: the cancellation of the August 1959 order of the Minister of Defense—limiting the granting and renewal of student deferments—and the defense of students affected by the decree; the moral victory gained when the courts granted UNEF's contention that the Minister of Education had illegally awarded to the Fédération Nationale des Etudiants de France seats on the Administrative Council of the Centre National des Oeuvres in 1961; the cancellation of rent increases in university housing after rent strikes and demonstrations in December 1963; and the decision of the Minister of Education to construct emergency facilities for the Faculty of Letters in Paris after the manifestations of discontent at the Sorbonne in 1963–1964.

The cost of these victories, however, has been very high. Three basic propositions were advanced in Chapter 1. They were: (1) that student organizations with a high degree of autonomy from nonstudent hierarchies are more dependent upon a favorable external context than are interest associations composed of almost any other category of people, (2) that, under conditions of political stability, the indulgence of decision-makers is the most important single determinant of the power of such organizations, and (3) that the adoption of specific noncorporate political positions by a relatively successful corporate interest group entails a high risk of compromising the total effectiveness of the group. Let us reconsider these propositions in regard to the experience of UNEF.

The last proposition would apply to any corporate interest group. To take controversial positions on noncorporate issues risks internal dissension and the alienation of potential sources of external support. During the first period of minoritaire control, 1946 to 1950, the yearly increase in the membership of UNEF was almost equal to the yearly increase during the corporatist period, 1950 to 1956. During the 1940's and early 1950's, however, the debate whether UNEF should be student oriented or student and environment oriented remained on a rather theoretical level. Though the advocates of the latter type of organization tended to be on the left of the political spectrum, there was no single political issue over which opinion within UNEF, or in the society at large, could violently polarize. The advocates of both orientations were able to compete in the one organization and to accept the preferences of the majority.

The Algerian issue polarized both French society and the student milieu. The question of orientation was no longer posed on the theoretical level. It was now a question of conscience and, for the minoritaires, a question of the performance or betrayal of the obligations of young intellectuals to society. Many of the corporatists were just as intensely committed to the French presence in Algeria as the minoritaires were to a termination of the war and the granting of self-determination. Despite the fact that the minoritaires hesitated to assert a firm position on the war, some majoritaire dissidents left the organization in 1957; but, not finding the expected support for their action on the part of the government, they reentered UNEF in 1958. The fighting intensified, and the use of torture by the French military and police in Algeria became established practice. By 1960 the minoritaires decided that the defection of some corporatists was preferable to continued silence on the basic issue. UNEF called for an end to the fighting and for the negotiation of self-determination for Algeria.

The decision cost UNEF the support of an important segment of the corporatists. Given the configuration of attitudes, however, defection on one side or the other was inevitable. For both antagonists the very legitimacy of the organization was at stake. A similar pattern was evidenced in the dissension and defections which the United States National Student Association recently experienced over the issues of civil rights and Vietnam.

A loss of membership is never pleasant for an organization. It entails some diminution of resources such as money, manpower, and votes, and damage to its public image of truly representing the category of people it claims to represent. The most damaging consequence of UNEF's engagement on the Algerian issue, however, was the alienation of the governmental decision-making structure. This relates to our first and second propositions, that student organizations with a high degree of autonomy from non-student hierarchies are more dependent upon a favorable external context than are interest associations composed of almost any other category of people and that, under conditions of political stability, the indulgence of decision-makers is the most important determinant of the power of such organizations.

That UNEF's antiwar activities alienated decision-makers who were responsible for the prosecution of the Algerian War is understandable. What made the assumption of a position on the war especially dangerous for UNEF was that the same highly cohesive set of decision-makers was responsible for both the war and education policy. Moreover, the Gaullists were not known for their predisposition to indulge interest groups of any nature. On the contrary, one of the characteristics of the Gaullists was a Rousseauist antipathy toward all intermediary groups in the political process.[1] The probabilities were thus very high that UNEF's engagement on the Algerian War and related issues would arouse the government to take punitive measures which would adversely affect UNEF's effectiveness as a corporate interest group.

After the war the minoritaire leadership attempted to regain that influence in the corporate domain which UNEF had exerted before the war. At the Congresses of 1962 and 1963, those minoritaires who advocated an aggressively anti-Gaullist policy were defeated by moderates who favored a policy of attempting to open up channels of access through persuasion and bargaining. At both Congresses the major policy decisions were limited to corporate issues: student housing, scholarships, and pedagogy.

Despite the overwhelming victory of the moderates and the

almost exclusive focus upon corporate issues at the 1962 Congress, the government maintained its policy of withholding funds and attention during the academic year 1962–1963. At the Congress of 1963 the moderate outgoing president, Jean-Claude Roure, admitted that the attempts of the National Bureau to open the channels of access had been in vain. Though he had been elected only one year before by a very large majority, his report to the 1963 Congress was almost not accepted. And the moderate candidate for the presidency, Michel Mousel, encountered stiff competition from and almost lost to a more militant candidate.

Two interacting forces were responsible for the growing militancy. One was the open confrontation of two opposed attitudes within the minoritaire movement which had emerged from the Algerian War period. One current of thought, represented by both Roure and Mousel and overwhelmingly dominant at the 1962 Congress, believed in a relatively large degree of autonomy of corporate and noncorporate political issues. The representatives of this attitude did not deny that the educational system was an integral part of the total social and political system or that UNEF should take positions on noncorporate issues. But they did maintain that the organization had a primarily corporate vocation and that, with the termination of the war, the issues most important to the French student body were their living and working conditions. To deal with these issues, they insisted, the organization needed access to decision-makers. They felt that open manifestations of hostility toward the regime would not be helpful in securing this access.

The attitude opposed to this was what eventually came to be known as the Syndical Left. Those who subscribed to it conceived of a greater fusion of corporate and political issues. Attacking the majority minoritaires for "neo-corporatism," this very small minority at the 1962 Congress tended to view UNEF as essentially an environment-oriented organization. In their eyes, student issues, no matter how concrete, had to be viewed within a broader ideological perspective. Demands concerned purely with corporate self-interest were regarded as illegitimate. This approach represented a much higher degree of alienation from the social and political system than did the other. Its adherents were almost alone in advocating a militantly anti-Gaullist position at the 1962 Congress; by 1963 they were almost a majority.

The second and more crucial force was the general sense of impatience, frustration, and hostility generated within UNEF by the refusal of the government to recognize them during the academic year 1962–1963. Among the more vocal advocates of a militantly anti-Gaullist policy at the 1963 Congress were members of the Union des Etudiants Communistes. While only one member of the UEC was elected to the National Bureau at the Congress of 1962, three were elected to the Mousel Bureau in 1963. By this time it was fairly obvious that the continuation of the policy of moderation depended heavily on the ability of the Mousel Bureau to secure corporate gains. And here the moderates were completely at the mercy of the government. The decision of Minister of Education Fouchet to restore UNEF's subsidy after the 1963 Congress gave the moderates some temporary hope that their approach would be successful.

If the sole or major interest of the government was to see a depolitization of UNEF, as M. Fouchet's speech before the National Assembly on 21 November 1964 would seem to indicate, the strategy adopted by the government during the academic year 1963–1964 was ill-adapted to its objectives. The authoritarian measures adopted at the beginning of the year—the reduction of student representation on the Administrative Council of the Centre National des Oeuvres, the rejection of student demands, and the attempt to suppress with force the students' public expression of discontent—had quite the contrary effect. They resulted in an increased politization and radicalization of the organization.

By the second semester of the 1963–1964 academic year, resentment against the government was so intense that the moderate National Bureau almost completely lost control over the activities of the more radical AGES. This was clearly demonstrated by the crisis which we have referred to as the Segni Affair. Held approximately two months after the affair, UNEF's 1964 Congress reflected a much higher degree of antiregimist sentiment than had the two previous Congresses. Six, or just over one-third of the members of the National Bureau elected at the Congress, were members of the Union des Etudiants Communistes, and the delegates voted to affiliate as a regular member with the communist-controlled International Union of Students.[2] Five months later, at the General Assembly of September, the organization accepted the propositions of the Syndical Left.

Keeping in mind the two opposing tendencies which are characteristic of student activists in both France and the United States—the striving for independence, and the striving for effectiveness—the reaction of the students to the government's strategy was predictable and understandable. It was hypothesized in Chapter 1 that the desire for a high degree of independence from nonstudent hierarchies is stronger in student organizations in older and relatively stable political communities. This tendency is especially strong in France, where it is also a reaction against the extremely authoritarian nature of the French family and school. To a great extent French student activism is an experience in liberation and collective self-assertion. While the return to an almost exclusive preoccupation with corporate issues in 1962 and 1963 appeared to most minoritaires reasonable and desirable if adopted voluntarily by the students, the attempt of the government to dictate this policy rendered it unacceptable. The Gaullist regime became one more authoritarian nonstudent hierarchy against which the students felt the need to rebel.

Thus, even if the government had held out the promise of effectiveness in the corporate domain, it would have been difficult for the activists to have moved in the desired direction so long as stringent negative sanctions were applied or threatened. However, even the moderates became convinced that no such *quid pro quo* would be forthcoming. The decision of M. Fouchet to reduce the representation of all student organizations, the FNEF as well as UNEF, on the Administrative Council of the CNO convinced most of the students that the government had no real intention of allowing them any voice in matters of education and student welfare. Under these conditions any formal commitment to the government would have been understood as a betrayal of the Charter of Grenoble and a surrender of independence without a corresponding gain in effectiveness in the corporate domain.

There was nothing UNEF could have done to regain its direct influence in the policy process. However, the problem of independence from nonstudent hierarchies was not solved by the refusal of the organization to capitulate to the government. Because of the limited resources available to student organizations, UNEF was presented with the choice of seriously curtailing its activities or seeking financial assistance from other external sources. The latter path was chosen and, by January 1967, UNEF had incurred debts amounting to almost $100,000.

As of July 1964 the most important creditors were labor and teachers organizations with left-wing anti-Gaullist orientations. The student leadership was well aware of the potential loss of independence involved in accumulating large debts. In an attempt to minimize the risk, they sought assistance from both communist-oriented (the Confédération Générale du Travail) and noncommunist or anticommunist organizations (the Fédération de l'Education Nationale, the Syndicat National des Instituteurs, and the laic Ligue Française de l'Enseigment). They also tried to avoid borrowing a disproportionate sum from any one source.[3]

It has been maintained and demonstrated that, in a confrontation of force between student organizations and the government, the students stand very little chance of emerging victorious. The exception to this is where students are prepared, or convince political decision-makers that they are prepared, to engage in revolutionary activity in countries with a high degree of political instability. And even under these conditions students require support from powerful nonstudent sources. In any case this kind of situation pertains neither in France nor in the United States. In this sense there is little reason for the general population in either country to be haunted by the spectre of student activism.

But decision-makers who rely exclusively or primarily upon their ability to cut off channels of access and to stifle by force the articulation of grievances court consequences which they are likely to regret. While one might not expect the Gaullist government to regret the incapacitation of UNEF as a viable interest group, its policy in regard to the students has had other effects which the government must accept with less equanimity.

The first is that a substantial segment of the student population has been alienated from the Gaullist regime. As has been indicated, the policies of the government undercut the moderates' control of

UNEF, and the leadership had to seek financial support from non-student hierarchies hostile to the government. But resentment over the tactics of the government and its lack of adequate concern for serious educational and student problems was not limited to the members or activists of UNEF. Discontent tended to spread widely within the student milieu. Even the FNEF, which had enjoyed the sponsorship of the Gaullists as a rival of UNEF, openly expressed resentment over the levels of expenditure devoted to education and the reduction of the student voice in decisions affecting their own welfare.

The most dramatic sign of alienation within the student culture has been the rise of independent, antiregimist, environment-oriented organizations, which has coincided with the decline in importance of UNEF. In the summer of 1966, two right-wing student groups conducted training courses in nationalism and karaté. When the school year commenced the members of right- and left-wing student organizations engaged each other in serious physical battles, bringing the university community under what *Le Monde* has called "The Reign of Violence." [4] Because of its immobilization as an effective interest group, UNEF no longer exerts the same issue-oriented, moderating influence upon student politics that it did during the Fourth Republic and the Algerian War. Furthermore, the effective use of violence by the government to suppress manifestations of student discontent has contributed in no small measure to the increasing resort to violence on the part of students.

Second, in both the educational and the civic domains the government has deprived itself of an important source of information by losing contact with what still remains the most representative student association in the nation. The attempt of the government to maintain contact with the student world through a rival structure, which it helped create, has not been successful. Clark Kerr, who has had more exposure to intense student activism than most other American educators in the postwar period, has stated:

To lose contact with the mind of youth . . . is to lose contact with a particularly revealing aspect of reality. As goes youth, so may go the nation—only more slowly and less completely. It [youth] moves with the tides of national life, and at some recent times, in the vanguard.[5]

Indeed, there are some recent indications that the government is adopting a more positive attitude toward UNEF. In the summer of 1966 the Ministry of Education issued a very attractively designed report on the educational reforms being implemented by M. Fouchet. On the top half of the inside cover appears a large photograph of M. Fouchet talking amiably with students at UNEF's cultural festival. In the January 1967 issue of *Education in France,* a publication of the Cultural Services of the French Embassy in the United States, there appeared an article on the need for civic education in France. The article is prefaced by a large and flattering photograph of UNEF's officers standing on the balcony of the organization's headquarters. The caption of the photograph reads, in an apparently admiring vein, "Are the students the only ones these days who are engaged in politics?" Before his appointment to the Ministry of the Interior in 1967, M. Fouchet had begun discussion with the leaders of UNEF about resumption of relations and the subsidy. However, the two sides were never able to arrive at a meeting of minds.

Given the failure of the Syndical Left to apply its confrontation theories, UNEF's shift to a less bellicose orientation, a national leadership dominated by members and sympathizers of the PSU, the increasing strength of the majoritaires in Paris, and the new leadership at the Ministry of Education, it is quite possible that UNEF's leaders and the government will arrive at a mutual accommodation. Even if the organization should come under majoritaire leadership, however, it is extremely doubtful that the activists would be willing to pay the price of a dictated narrowed orientation in order to regain the subsidy and open the channels of communication. Should the Gaullists remain in power for any length of time and should they maintain the policy of blockage which is entirely within their capabilities, UNEF will probably continue to experience some decline in membership and severe frustration and internal conflict.

It is doubtful, however, that the organization will disintegrate entirely. Its long history, spanning three French republics and the

Vichy regime, and its past performances and public recognition have given the organization a cushion of legitimacy and support within the student milieu and the general society. While the statistics would seem to indicate some improvement in the material living and working conditions of students under the Fourth Economic Plan, there are stimuli for student activism still deeply rooted in the French socio-cultural and educational systems, and these show little prospect of disappearing in the near future. While there are certain tendencies which more or less clearly differentiate activists on the basis of their orientations, the propensity to engage in activism is well diffused throughout the student culture.

Moreover, UNEF continues to receive crucial support and encouragement from left-wing parties, unions, and the left-of-center press. We have already noted the financial assistance which UNEF has received from teachers and labor organizations. Parliamentarians of both the SFIO and the Communist Party have been staunch in their defense of UNEF in the National Assembly. In the national elections of 1967 both the Federation of the Left and the Parti Socialiste Unifié included UNEF's proposal for an *allocation d'études* in their platforms. The shadow-cabinet minister of education of the Federation was an old friend of UNEF, René Billières. Billières, the last minister of education of the Fourth Republic and the first minister of education of the Fifth Republic, strongly supported UNEF when it came under attack in governmental circles during the schism of 1957 and 1958. And it was UNEF's support of Billières' reform proposals which first brought the organization into conflict with the Gaullists. Far from the least important source of support has been the extensive, generally sympathetic treatment which UNEF has received from two organs of the French press, the left-of-center and influential *Le Monde* and the further left *Nouvel-Observateur*. There is little doubt that if the left were to come to power, UNEF would regain both its subsidy and much, if not all, of its former influence as a corporate interest group.

The most remarkable testimony to the staying power of UNEF is that, as late as the academic year 1966–1967, the organization could still attract a voluntary membership of approximately 50,000 students and that the two-party system has been experiencing a revitalization in the form of *majoritaire* victories in Parisian AGES.

Even while it has remained stripped of almost all direct influence upon education policy, UNEF continues to provide a structure which meets strongly felt needs for expression and participation within the French student milieu.

NOTES

1. See Jean Meynaud, "Les Groupes de pression sous la Ve République," *Revue Française de Science Politique*, XII, No. 3 (September 1962), 672–697.
2. See Chapter 4, pp. 91–93 of this work.
3. In an interview with the author in 1968, Jacques Sauvageot, vice-president of UNEF, claimed that the organization had liquidated its debts to these organizations and maintained that its $100,000 obligation was to "private" creditors from whom UNEF purchased services. Interview of 20 June 1968.
4. *Le Monde*, 9 December 1966, p. 9.
5. Clark Kerr, "From Apathy to Confrontation" (address delivered before the Congress on Students and Politics at the University of Puerto Rico, 25 March 1967).

Chapter 8

Postscript: UNEF and the Student Revolt of May–June 1968

With the exception of updated data in certain sections, the preceding pages were completed before the confrontations of May and June 1968. Currents and trends in student politics are so susceptible to rapid changes that it is futile to attempt more fully to update lengthy studies in order to account for every late development. However, the revolt of May and June was of such an extraordinary nature and attracted so much attention throughout the world that something should be said about UNEF's role in it, its implications for the future of UNEF, and its bearing upon the hypotheses, observations, and predictions contained in this work.[1]

It is still too soon after the event to assess fully the significance of the revolt. It might well be that the extraordinary consciousness and activism to which it gave rise will prove the necessary catalyst for important change across a wide range of French institutions. While we do predict such change, we shall here restrict ourselves to considering only the results already realized.

The students were not able to bring about the immediate collapse of the regime, and the Gaullists were able to parlay the confrontations into a stunning electoral victory in June. But the revolt did result in extremely important victories for the students. Let us deal briefly with these accomplishments.

Two positive changes were achieved at the time of the confrontations.[2] The first was the removal of the most unfavorable decision-makers and their replacement with more favorable officials. The Gaullists who had been largely responsible for the hard line taken against UNEF since the inception of the Fifth Republic and who had assumed the same posture against the students in the early stages of the confrontations were dismissed from the cabinet. Dismissed were: Minister of Education Alain Peyrefitte, who took a hard line during the 1968 confrontations and who, as Minister of Information in 1963 and 1964, had censored television coverage of the police driving the students off the streets and had been responsible for the hostile coverage of UNEF; Minister of Justice Louis Joxe, who opposed any amnesty for or intervention in behalf of arrested students during the 1968 confrontations and who, as minister of education in 1960, first suspended UNEF's subsidy; and Christian Fouchet, minister of education during our period of field work, who subsequently became minister of interior, in which capacity he ordered the police and CRS into action against the students during the 1968 confrontations. Another long-time hard-liner involved in determining the government's response to the students in 1968 was Michel Debré, minister of finance, who had often been discussed as the probable successor of de Gaulle; he was shifted to the Ministry of Foreign Affairs, removing him from all responsibility in domestic policy. René Capitant, one of the two Gaullist deputies who resigned their seats in the National Assembly to protest the hard-liners' handing of the situation, replaced Joxe in the Ministry of Justice. And the Ministry of Education was turned over to a non-Gaullist sympathetic with the student grievances, Edgar Faure, twice Radical Socialist premier during the Fourth Republic.

The second favorable outcome of the confrontations was the commitment of the government to fundamental educational reforms along the lines advocated by UNEF. The two key elements of the promised reforms are the decentralization of the system of higher education, so that each university will possess a high degree of autonomy, and the creation of governing bodies in which students will be represented.

Another important outcome occurred ten months after the actual confrontations. This was General de Gaulle's defeat on the April 1969 referendum and his subsequent retirement from public life. Although it has been argued that the General needlessly put himself in so vulnerable a position, the fact is that he did do so, and that both his decision to hold the referendum and the French electorate's loss of confidence in him were determined by the events of May and June. Thus, while their "Adieu de Gaulle" was premature in May 1968, the students did play a decisive role in eliminating from public office the man they saw as their primary adversary.

In light of these accomplishments, the major theoretical question is whether or not we have underestimated the potential political power of students. Two factors deserve consideration here.

First, this work is the study of an organization. It is concerned with the attempt by students to exert power on a continuing basis through organizational structures. Far from indicating the final success of such activity, the student revolt was the most graphic result of its failure.

At both the national and local levels, UNEF's role in the catalytic processes which touched off the revolt was minimal. Moreover, the revolt completely shattered the structure of UNEF. The National Bureau, which did supply a degree of coordination and direction to the revolt after it was already under way, was completely cut off from the local AGES. Indeed, many of the chapters had been dissolved by the militants and replaced by "action committees" or "occupation committees." A student who defined UNEF during the revolt as "four men around a telephone" came very close to describing the literal reality. It is interesting, however, that the calls to action issued by UNEF's national officers were accorded a high degree of legitimacy among the students, despite the fact that the structure had collapsed.

While a good many student organizations were involved in the events of May and June in one way or another, the revolt cannot be explained as the result of organizational activity. Rather, the revolt was a massive and highly spontaneous explosion of the strong antiregimist sentiments which existed within the student milieu. We have already discussed the basic sources of discontent. The immediate stimulus which triggered the revolt was the closing of the Nanterre campus and its occupation by the police, followed by the arrest of between five and six hundred students (including most prominent student leaders in the country) when they met at the Sorbonne to discuss the situation at Nanterre. As we have indicated, antiregimist sentiment had reached dangerous levels throughout the student world as early as 1964. While one would have had to resort to supernatural devices in order to predict in 1964 that a student uprising of massive dimensions would take place in May and June 1968, it was reasonable then to assume that if the government continued to remain insensitive to these sentiments, they would somehow manifest themselves in overt behavior. UNEF as an organization posed no threat to the government. But the continued alienation of a very large segment of the student population did.

Second, we must recall our hypothesis that student organizations stand little chance of emerging victorious in a confrontation with a determined government unless (1) they are prepared to engage in revolutionary activity or convince political decision-makers that they are, (2) there is a high degree of political instability, and (3) they enjoy the support of powerful nonstudent forces. In stating these conditions we were influenced by the prior experience of UNEF and by two cases of political change in which students had been instrumental, the overthrow of the Rhee regime in South Korea and of Sukarno in Indonesia. We contended that this kind of situation existed neither in France nor the United States. Setting aside for the moment the fact that we were referring to student organizations and that the French student revolt was largely a spontaneous and extraorganizational effort, let us discuss the conditions of the hypothesis and the realities of May and June.

What happened was that the conditions of the hypothesis unfolded in a causal sequence. Condition (1) appeared first. The anger generated by the actions and responses of the government, added to the deep antiregimist sentiments already present within the student world, led to a situation where the toppling of the regime became a major objective of the revolt. And the political decision-makers were painfully aware of this.

Next appeared condition (3), the support of powerful nonstudent sources. The most sustained sources of support were the Syndicat National de l'Enseignement Supérieur (a university teachers union which claims the membership of approximately one-third of the academics in France) and the Parti Socialiste Unifié. In the early stages of the confrontations, the labor movement and an important segment of Parisian public opinion sided with the students. After the police and paramilitary CRS engaged the students in battle and finally succeeded in destroying the barricades on the night of May 10, all of the major labor confederations joined the students and teachers in calling a twenty-four-hour strike and in putting between 500,000 and one million demonstrators in the streets of Paris on the 13th.

The most important support, however, came when between nine and ten million workers went on wildcat strikes, seized major industrial complexes, and brought the productive and distributive processes of the country to a halt. Whether a significant percentage of the workers had any interest in the problems and aims of the students or saw the student revolt simply as a fortuitous occasion to take action in their own interest makes little difference in regard to the effect of their actions. The workers were inspired by the example of the students, there was a sharply antiregimist tenor to their activities, and within the total power configuration the students and the striking workers were *de facto* allies.

The result of the actions of the students and workers was the appearance of condition (2). The government was rendered incapable of performing most of its functions or even of suppressing the students and was placed on the verge of collapse. Moreover, even after the workers had gone back to their jobs, the situation was potentially still so volatile that the government could ill afford to reverse itself on the concessions granted to the students. Thus, while it is true that there existed underlying discontent among the workers (as among other segments of the French population) which made the process possible, it was the students themselves who set off the chain reaction which put the government and regime in immanent danger of collapse. Had the students not risen up, this observer doubts very much that the workers would have done so or that the political system would have been in any serious jeopardy in the foreseeable future. And, as we hope this work has amply demonstrated, it is just as doubtful that the students would have experienced any success in extracting concessions from the government.

Despite the student victories UNEF is now facing its toughest challenge. Ironically, the confrontation and mobilization of students which was responsible for the at least partial satisfaction of demands long articulated in vain by UNEF resulted in the complete collapse of the organization's structure. Instead of attempting to call a Congress in the summer of 1968, UNEF's National Bureau called a national meeting (Les Assises Nationales de l'UNEF) and publicly requested every Parisian faculty and provincial university to send one delegate to represent each thousand students enrolled. No guidelines were presented for the selection of delegates. Quite predictably, the meeting was chaotic and no decisions were reached.

However, within the context of the revolt, the destruction of the old structure was viewed as a necessity even by the national leaders. One major theme of the revolt was participation, and never before in French history had such a large number of students participated in a political event. The hope of UNEF's leaders was that a high level of participation could be sustained in the future. And it was generally agreed that the hierarchical structure of UNEF not only could not accommodate a mobilized mass of students but would indeed serve to stifle participation.

Moreover, the decentralization of the educational decision-making process will significantly change the rules of the game. For if the powers of decision-making are truly decentralized, it would no longer be rational for a national apparatus supported by local AGES to concentrate the resources of the organization upon a single and easily identifiable set of officials in Paris. Thus the search is on for new forms of organization, compatible with decentralization and the philosophy of participatory democracy, which will, at the same time, preserve a feeling of solidarity among students throughout the nation and serve as a channel of articulation for student sentiment on important national and international issues.

NOTES

1. See my "The Revolution Betrayed: The French Student Revolt of May–June 1968," in Seymour Martin Lipset and Philip Altbach, eds., *Students in Revolt* (Boston: Houghton Mifflin, 1969), pp. 127–166.
2. While not of the same order of significance, the students also won an amnesty on May 22 for all who had participated in the demonstrations and clashes with the police.

Glossary

ACJF	Association Catholique de la Jeunesse Française. Catholic youth association under the Church hierarchy with which the Jeunesse Etudiante Chrétienne (JEC) is affiliated.
ACU	Action Catholique Universitaire. A Catholic student organization with close ties to the hierarchy created in 1966.
AGE	Association Générale des Etudiants. The local chapters of UNEF.
CFTC	Confédération Française des Travailleurs Chrétiens. France's second largest labor confederation, of progressive Catholic inspiration. In 1964 there was a split and the majority faction now refers to itself as the Confédération Française et Démocratique du Travail (CFDT).
CGT	Confédération Générale du Travail. France's largest labor confederation; communist led.
CGT-FO	Confédération Générale du Travail-Force Ouvriève. France's third largest labor confederation; anticommunist socialist orientation.
CLER	Comité de Liaison des Etudiants Révolutionnaires. A Trotskyist (Lambertist brand) student organization formed in 1961 and affiliated with the tiny Parti Communiste Internationaliste. In 1968 its name was changed to the Fédération des Etudiants Revolutionnaires and then to the Comité pour la Défense de l'UNEF.
CND	The Campaign for Nuclear Disarmament in Britain.
CNO	Centre National des Oeuvres en Faveur de la Jeunesse Scolaire et Universitaire. The organization which makes policy and administers in the area of student benefits.

CRS   Compagnies Républicaines de Sécurité. A para-military police force.

FEN   Fédération de l'Education Nationale. A teachers' confederation which groups teachers' unions at the primary, secondary, and university levels.

FLN   Front de Libération Nationale. The Algerian liberation movement which fought the French.

FNEF   Fédération Nationale des Etudiants de France. UNEF's smaller rival student union.

FUJP   Force Unies de la Jeunesse Patriotique. A resistance youth alliance during World War II.

ISC   International Student Conference. An international student organization created in 1950 with the assistance of the CIA to counter the communist controlled International Union of Students.

IUS   International Union of Students. An international student organization created in 1948. Controlled by the Communist Party of the Soviet Union.

JCR   Jeunesse Communiste Révolutionnaire. A Trotskyist (Frankist brand) student organization created in 1967. It is not affiliated with any political party.

JEC   Jeunesse Etudiante Chrétienne. A Catholic student organization created in 1929. See ACJF.

JUC   Jeunesse Universitaire Chrétienne. A Catholic student organization created in 1965–1966. It has no ties with the Church.

MRP   Mouvement Républicain Populaire. A Catholic political party shattered and ultimately destroyed by the Algerian War.

OAS   Organisation de l'Armée Secrète. The underground fighting network which stood for the continued French presence in Algeria.

PSA   Parti Socialiste Autonome. See PSU.

PSU   Parti Socialiste Unifié. Relatively small socialist party created by the merger in 1960 of two smaller parties, the Parti Socialiste Autonome (PSA) and the Union de la Gauche Socialiste (UGS). Both the PSA and the UGS were created in 1958.

SFIO   Section Française de l'Internationale Ouvrière. The major French socialist party.

SGEN   Syndicat Général de l'Education Nationale. A teachers' union, grouping teachers at all levels, affiliated with the CFTC (now with the CFDT).

SNESup. Syndicat National de l'Ensiegnement Supérieur. The university teachers' union affiliated with the Fédération de l'Education Nationale (FEN).

UGS Union de la Gauche Socialiste. See PSU.

UNEF Union Nationale des Etudiants de France. France's largest student union.

UEC Union des Etudiants Communistes. Student affiliate of the French Communist Party.

UGEMA Union Générale des Etudiants Musulmans Algériens. The nationalistic Algerian Arab student union.

UJCML Union des Jeunesses Communistes (Marxiste-Leniniste). A pro-Chinese communist student organization created in 1966.

USNSA United States National Student Association. The larger of the two American associations of student governments.

Bibliography

Books and Pamphlets

L'Année politique, économique, sociale, et diplomatique en France 1963. Paris: Presses Universitaires de France, 1964.

L'Année politique, économique, sociale, et diplomatique en France 1964. Paris: Presses Universitaires de France, 1965.

L'Année politique, économique, sociale, et diplomatique en France 1965. Paris: Presses Universitaires de France, 1966.

Aron, Raymond. *The Opium of the Intellectuals.* Translated by Terence Kilmartin. New York: The Norton Library, 1962.

Barrès, Maurice. *Scènes et doctrines du nationalisme,* Vol. I. Paris: Librairie Plon, 1925.

De Beauvoir, Simone. *La Force des choses.* Paris: Gallimard, 1963.

Benda, Julian. *The Betrayal of the Intellectuals.* Translated by Richard Aldington. Boston: The Beacon Press, 1955.

Bodin, Louis. *Les Intellectuels.* Paris: Presses Universitaires de France, 1962.

Bourdet, Claude. *Les Chemins de l'unité.* Paris: Maspero, 1964.

Bourdieu, Pierre, and Passeron, Jean-Claude. *Les Etudiants et leurs études.* Paris: Mouton, 1964.

————. *Les Héritiers: les étudiants et la culture.* Paris: Editions de Minuit, 1964.

Brombert, Victor. *The Intellectual Hero: Studies in the French Novel 1880–1955.* Philadelphia: J. B. Lippincott Company, 1960.

Caute, David. *Communism and the French Intellectuals 1914–1960.* London: André Deutsch, 1964.

Conseil Français des Mouvements de Jeunesse. *Présence de la jeunesse.* Paris: Privat, 1955.

Dahl, Robert A. *A Preface to Democratic Theory.* Chicago: The University of Chicago Press, 1956.

Dahl, Robert A., and Lindblom, Charles. *Politics, Economics, and Welfare.* New York: Harper & Row, 1953.

Delhorbe, Cecile. *L'Affaire Dreyfus et les écrivains français.* Neuchatel: Editions Victor Attinger, 1923.

Eckstein, Harry. *Pressure Group Politics: The Case of the British Medical Association.* Stanford: Stanford University Press, 1960.

Finer, S. K. *Anonymous Empire.* London: Pall Mall Press, 1958.

De la Fournière, Michel, and Borella, François. *Le Syndicalisme étudiant.* Paris: Editions du Seuil, 1957.

Franceschi, Joseph. *Les Groupes de pression dans la defense de l'enseignement public.* Paris: Libraires Techniques, 1964.

Fraser, W. R. *Education and Society in Modern France.* London: Routledge & Kegan Paul, 1963.

The Gangrene. Translated by Robert Silvers. New York: Lyle Stuart, 1960.

Gau, Jacques. *Le Régime de sécurité sociale des étudiants.* Paris: Librairie Générale de Droit et de Jurisprudence, 1960.

Gaudez, Pierre. *Les Etudiants.* Paris: Julliard, 1961.

Girod de l'Ain, Bertrand. *Le Réforme de l'enseignement supérieur.* Paris: Le Monde, 1964.

Hautmont, Nicole. *Habitat et vie étudiant.* Paris: Mutuelle Nationale des Etudiants de France, 1963.

Kanapa, Jean. *Situation de l'intellectuel.* Paris: Editions Sociales, 1957.

Lipset, S. M., Trow, M., and Coleman, J. *Union Democracy.* Garden City: Anchor Books, 1962.

Lipset, S. M., and Wolin, S., eds. *The Berkeley Revolt.* Garden City: Anchor Books, 1965.

Meynaud, Jean. *Les Groupes de pression en France.* Paris: Cahiers de la Fondation Nationale des Sciences Politiques, Librairie Armand Colin, 1958.

————. *Nouvelles Etudes sur les groupes de pression en France.* Paris: Cahiers de la Fondation Nationale des Sciences Politiques, Librairie Armand Colin, 1962.

Meynaud, Jean, and Lancelot, Alain. *Le Participation des français à la politique.* Paris: Presses Universitaires de France, 1961.

Michel, Henri. *Histoire de la Résistance en France.* Paris: Presses Universitaires de France, 1962.

Michels, Robert. *Political Parties.* Translated by Eden and Cedar Paul. Glencoe: The Free Press, 1958.

Miller, M. V., and Gilmore, S., eds. *Revolution at Berkeley.* New York: Dell, 1965.

Paleologue, Maurice. *Journal de l'Affaire Dreyfus 1894–1899: l'Affaire Dreyfus et le Quai d'Orsay.* Paris: Plon, 1955.

Péguy, Charles. *De la Situation faite à l'histoire et à la sociologie dans les temps modernes.* In *Oeuvres complètes de Charles Péguy,* Vol. III. Paris: Editions de la Nouvelle Revue Française, 1927.

————. *Notre Jeunesse.* In *Oeuvres complètes de Charles Péguy,* Vol. III. Paris: Editions de la Nouvelle Revue Française, 1927.

Perche, Louis. *Essai sur Charles Péguy.* Paris: Pierre Seghers, 1957.

Le Plan Langevin–Wallon de réforme de l'enseignement. Paris: Presses Universitaires de France, 1964.

Ribon, Florence. *Condition des étudiants.* Paris: Tendences, 1967.

Thibaudet, Albert. *La République des professeurs.* Paris: Grasset, 1927.

Truman, David. *The Governmental Process.* New York: Alfred A. Knopf, 1951.

Zinn, Howard. *SNCC: The New Abolitionists.* Boston: Beacon Press, 1964.

Essays and Articles

Almond, Gabriel A. "Introduction: A Functional Approach to Comparative Politics." In Gabriel A. Almond and James B. Coleman, eds., *The Politics of the Developing Areas.* Princeton: Princeton University Press, 1960, pp. 3–64.

L'Aurore, 15 January 1898, p. 1.

L'Aurore, 16 January 1898, p. 2.

Barale, Jean. "Les Etudiants d'Aix-en-Provence." *Revue Française de Science Politique*, XII, No. 3 (September 1962), 964–982.

Barrès, Maurice. "La Protestation des intellectuels!" *Le Journal*, 1953 (1 February 1898), 1.

Bodin, Louis et Touchard, Jean. "Les Intellectuels dans la société française contemporaine." *Revue Française de Science Politique*, IX, No. 4 (December 1959), 835–859.

Botsford, Keith. "Why Students in France Go Communist: Elite Proletarians All." *New York Times Magazine*, 13 November 1966, pp. 54–99.

Collinet, Michel. "Les Etudiants communistes français en révolte contre le parti." *Preuves-Informations* (Paris), 30 March 1965.

Copfermann, Emile. "Menaces sur les mouvements des jeunes." *Partisans*, VIII (January–February 1963), 83–91.

————. "Les Mouvements de jeunes, l'Etat et la jeunesse." *Perspectives Socialistes*, No. 47 (October 1961), 5–16.

"La Crise et l'avenir de la jeunesse universitaire." *Journal des Economistes* (September–October 1935), pp. 462–481.

Delcroix, François. "Les Etudiants dans le tunnel." *Le Nouvel Observateur*, 14 January 1965, pp. 1–2.

Denis, André. "Pour une Politique de la jeunesse." In *Récherches et Débats du Centre Catholique des Intellectuels Français: La France, Va-t-elle Perdre Sa Jeunesse?* Paris: Libraire Arthème Fayard, July 1954, pp. 36–41.

Duverger, Maurice. "Le Despotisme inefficace." *Le Monde*, 27–28 October 1963, p. 1.

Duvignaud, Jean. "L'Intervention des intellectuels dans la vie publique." *Arguments*, IV, No. 20 (summer 1960), 45–46.

Fields, A. Belden. "The Revolution Betrayed: The French Student Revolt of May–June 1968." In Seymour Martin Lipset and Philip Altbach, eds., *Students in Revolt*. Boston: Houghton Mifflin, 1969, pp. 127–166.

Fougeyrollas, Pierre. "Le Mot intellectuel." *Arguments*, IV, No. 20 (summer 1960), 47–49.

Frèyssinet, Jacques. "Où Vont les Etudiants?" *Cahiers de la République*, V (26 July–August 1960), 7–15.

Gallagher, Orvoell R. "Voluntary Associations in France." *Social Forces*, XXXVI, No. 2 (December 1957), 148–160.

Gaunez, Pierre. "L'Avenir de l'UNEF." *Partisans*, XIII (December 1963–January 1964), 205–211.

Girardet, Raoul. "Le Problème de l'engagement politique en milieu étudiant." In Georges Vedel, ed., *La Dépolitisation: mythe ou réalité?* Paris: Cahiers de la Fondation Nationale des Sciences Politiques, Librairie Armand Colin, 1962, pp. 269–274.

Girod de l'Ain, Bertrand. "L'Enseignement dans neuf pays 'développés.'" *Le Monde Sélection Hebdomadaire*, 10–16 March 1966, p. 7.

Griset, Antoine, and Kravetz, Marc. "De l'Algérie à la réforme Fouchet: critique du syndicalisme étudiant." *Les Temps Modernes*, No. 227 (April 1965), pp. 1880–1902, and No. 228 (May 1965), pp. 2066–2089.

Hoffmann, Stanley. "Paradoxes of the French Political Community." In Stanley Hoffmann, et al., *In Search of France*. Cambridge: Harvard University Press, 1963, pp. 1–117.

"Incident devant le petit écran." *Le Monde*, 7 April 1964, p. 9.

"Les Intellectuels at la politique." *France–Forum*, Vol. XLI (June 1962).

Jussieu, Marc. "ACJF: Historique d'une démission." *Esprit* (November 1956), pp. 694–696.

———. "ACJF: Signification d'une crise." *Esprit* (January 1956), pp. 116–125.

———. "Points de repère." *Esprit* (July–August 1957), pp. 78–83.

Kravetz, Marc. "Naissance d'un syndicalisme étudiant." *Les Temps Modernes*, No. 213 (February 1964), 1447–1475.

Lavau, Georges E. "Political Pressures by Interest Groups in France." In Henry W. Ehrmann, ed., *Interest Groups on Four Continents*. Pittsburgh: University of Pittsburgh Press, 1958, pp. 60–95.

Lipset, S. M., ed. *Comparative Education Review*. Special issue on student politics, X, No. 2 (June 1966), 129–376.

Litaudon, François. "Responses à un questionnaire." In *Récherches et Débats du Centre Catholique des Intellectuels Français*, No. 8, *La France, Va-t-elle Perdre Sa Jeunesse?* Paris: Librairie Arthème Fayard, July 1954, pp. 145–160.

Mazzola, Michel. "De l'Intellectuel chez Marx au Marxisme des intellectuels." *Arguments*, IV, No. 20 (summer 1960), 22–26.

Métraux, Rhoda. "Themes in French Culture." In Rhoda Métraux and Margaret Mead, *Themes in French Culture: A Preface to a Study of French Community*. Stanford: Stanford University Press, 1954, pp. 1–65.

Meynaud, Jean. "Essai d'analyse de l'influence des groupes d'intérêt." *Revue Economique*, No. 2 (1957), pp. 177–220.

———. "Les Groupes de pression sous la Ve République." *Revue Française de Science Politique*, XII, No. 3 (September 1962), 672–697.

Morin, Edgar. "Intellectuels: critique du mythe et mythe de la critique." *Arguments*, IV, No. 20 (summer 1960), 35–40.

Pascaud, Odette. "Etudiantes de Paris." *Revue des Deux Mondes* (May–June 1935), pp. 370–375.

Pinner, Frank A. "Student Trade-Unionism in France, Belgium, and Holland: Anticipatory Socialization and Role-Seeking." *Sociology of Education*, XXXVII, No. 3 (Spring 1964), 177–199.

Pitts, Jesse R. "Continuity and Change in Bourgeois France." In Stanley Hoffmann, et al., *In Seach of France*. Cambridge: Harvard University Press, 1963, pp. 235–304.

Remond, René. "Les Intellectuels el la politique." *Revue Française de Science Politique*, IX, No. 4 (December 1959), 860–880.

Rose, Arnold. "Voluntary Associations in France." In *Theory and Method in the Social Sciences*. Minneapolis: The University of Minnesota Press, 1954, pp. 72–115.

Shils, Edward. "Influence and Withdrawal: The Intellectuals in Indian Political Development." In Dwaine Marvick, ed., *Political Decision-Makers*. Glencoe: The Free Press, 1961, pp. 29–56.

———. "The Intellectuals and the Powers: Some Perspectives for Comparative Analysis." *Comparative Studies in Society and History* (October 1958), pp. 5–22.

Stern, Sol, et al. "NSA and the CIA." *Ramparts*, V, No. 9 (March 1967), 29–39.

Tomasson, Richard F. "From Elitism to Egalitarianism in Swedish Education." *Sociology of Education*, XXXVIII, No. 3 (Spring 1965), 204–223.

Van Landingham, Harry. "Special Correspondence: The Temper of French Post-War University Life." *School and Society*, XIV, No. 353 (1 October 1921), 250–253.

Worms, Jean-Pierre. "The French Student Movement." In S. M. Lipset, ed. *Student Politics*. Special issue of *The Comparative Education Review*, X, No. 2 (June 1966), 359–366.

Wylie, Laurence. "Youth in France and the United States." In Erik H. Erikson, ed. *The Challenge of Youth*. Garden City: Anchor Books, 1965, pp. 291–311.

Publications and Internal Documents of Student Organizations

"L'Affaire Paris-Science." *21.27: l'Etudiant de France* (publication of the Union Nationale des Etudiants de France), Numéro Spécial, 53e Congrès, p. 11.

Broche, François. "Le pape et Brigitte Bardot." *La France Etudiante* (publication of the Fédération Nationale des Etudiants de France), December 1963–January 1964, p. 12.

Chiffre, Alain. *Les Sources du syndicalisme étudiant depuis 1945*, Vol. II. Paris: Centre de Documentation, l'Union Nationale des Etudiants de France, 1963.

La Fédération Nationale des Etudiants de France, Association Corporative des Etudiants en Droit. *Projet de financement des études supérieures*. Paris, 1964.

La Fédération Nationale des Etudiants de France, Grenoble Chapter. *Le Marxisme dans l'Université*. Grenoble, 1965.

Kahn, Pierre. "Approfondir et Appliquer la Ligne du XXe Congrès."

Clarté (publication of the Union des Etudiants Communistes), No. 55 (March–April 1964), pp. 12–36.

Mareschal, François. "Le Pain quotidien." *Le Monde*, Numéro Spécial UNEF, 18 October 1963, p. 13.

Mousel, Michel. *Rapport Moral: 53ème Congrès de l'UNEF*, 1964.

Poitou, Gérard. "La Police, le pouvoir, et l'UNEF." *21·27: l'Etudiant de France*, No. 6 (March 1964), p. 43.

L'Union Nationale des Etudiants de France. *L'Allocation d'études*. Paris, 1965.

————. *Le Chartre.*

————. *Le 53e Congrès de l'UNEF* Transcripts. Paris: UNEF–Informations, 1964.

————. *Le 54e Congrès de l'UNEF* Transcripts. Paris: UNEF–Informations, 1965.

————. *Manifeste pour une réforme démocratique de l'enseignement supérieur.* Paris, 1964.

————. Official membership list, 1962–1963.

————. Official membership list, 1963–1964.

————. *Statutes.*

————. *UNEF–Informations, Données Statistiques, 53e Congrès.* Paris: UNEF–Informations, 1965.

————. *Un Seul Coeur.* Paris: January 1944.

United States National Student Association. *Statement of the National Supervisory Board.* 17 February 1967.

Government Documents and Publications

Aron, Robert. "The Faculty of Science at Orsay." *Education in France*, No. 28 (June 1965), pp. 9–10.

Fanton, André. *Journal Officiel de la République Française, Débats Parlementaires, Assemblée Nationale.* (Oral question to the Minister of Education on 21 November 1964.) November 1964, p. 5522.

————. *Journal Officiel de la République Française, Débats Parlementaires, Assemblée Nationale.* (Written question to the Minister of Education on 22 February 1964.) February 1964, p. 327.

Fouchet, Christian. Address before the *Inspection Générale*, 1 October 1964. Courtesy of The Service de Presse et de Relations Publiques, Ministère de l'Education Nationale.

————. *Journal Officiel de la République Française, Débats Parlementaires, Assemblée Nationale.* (Statement before the National Assembly, 21 November 1964.) November 1964, pp. 5522–5525.

François, Louis. "Civic Training in French Education." *Education in France*, No. 34 (January 1967), pp. 9–11.

French System of Education. Special issue of *Education in France*. Revised edition, 1965.

"Growth of Higher Education." *Education in France*, No. 28 (June 1965), pp. 5–8.

Institut National de la Statistique et des Etudes Economiques. *Annuaire statistique de la France. 1963 (Résultats de 1962)*. Paris, 1963.

———. *Tableaux de l'économie française*. Paris, 1963.

Journal Officiel de la République Française, Lois et Décrets. 17 April 1955, p. 3831.

Ministère de l'Education Nationale. *Evolution comparée des budgets de l'Etat et de l'éducation nationale depuis 1900*. Paris, 1963.

———. Service de Presse et de Relations Publiques. *Note d'information: la rentrée universitaire*. Paris, 1964.

———. *La Réforme de l'enseignement*. Paris, 1966.

"The Reform of French Education." *Education in France*, No. 32 (July 1966), pp. 1–10.

"The Reopening of Schools." *Education in France*, No. 23 (December 1963), pp. 1–4.

Unpublished Materials

Altbach, Edith. "Students in the Revolutions of 1848." Paper presented at the Conference on Students and Politics, San Juan, Puerto Rico, 27–31 March 1967.

Bachtiar, H. W. "Indonesian Students and Politics." Paper presented at the Conference on Students and Politics, San Juan, Puerto Rico, 27–31 March 1967.

Burnier, Michel-Antoine. "Les Existentialistes français et la vie politique 1945–1962." Thesis presented at the Institut d'Etudes Politiques in Paris, 1963.

Cornell, Richard. "Students and Politics in the Communist Countries of Eastern Europe." Paper presented at the Conference on Students and Politics, San Juan, Puerto Rico, 27–31 March 1967.

Davidson, Carl. "Toward a Student Syndicalist Movement or University Reform Revisited." Mimeographed paper presented at the Midwest Conference on Student Power, The University of Illinois, May 1967.

Fields, A. Belden. "The French Student Movement." Paper presented at the Conference on Students and Politics, San Juan, Puerto Rico, 27–31 March 1967.

Halsey, A. H., and Marks, Stephen. "British Student Politics." Paper presented at the Conference on Students and Politics, San Juan, Puerto Rico, 27–31 March 1967.

Kerr, Clark. "From Apathy to Confrontation." An address delivered before the Conference on Students and Politics at the University of Puerto Rico, 25 March 1967.

Lefèvre, Jacques François. "L'Union Nationale des Etudiants de France depuis 1945." Thesis submitted at the Institut d'Etudes Politiques in Paris, 1957–1958.

Pinner, Frank A. "Transition and Transgression: Some Characteristics of Student Movements in Western Europe." Paper presented at the Conference on Students and Politics, San Juan, Puerto Rico, 27–31 March 1967.

Shimberi, Michiya. "The Sociology of a Student Movement—A Japanese Case Study." Paper presented at the Conference on Students and Politics, San Juan, Puerto Rico, 27–31 March 1967.

Aside from the above sources, the numerous articles on student organizations and higher education which regularly appeared in *Le Monde* were of invaluable assistance.

Index